SCHOLASTIC

ALPHA Grammar and Composition

5

Anne Seaton
Series editor: Anne Seaton

About ALPHA™ Grammar and Composition

Welcome to **Scholastic ALPHA™ Grammar and Composition.**

This series comprises coursebooks for classes 1 to 5 and offers an easy, engaging and meaningful way to master the skills and mechanics of English **Grammar**, **Composition** and **Comprehension**.

Easy recall of prior topic followed by an exercise to check for readiness to learn

Grammar focus through an engaging picture story

Related exercises for meaningful learning

Simple definition to explain each grammar concept

Practice exercises for meaningful application of the concept

Periodic reviews to consolidate learning and for systematic assessment

Spot the Error to provide an opportunity for error correction

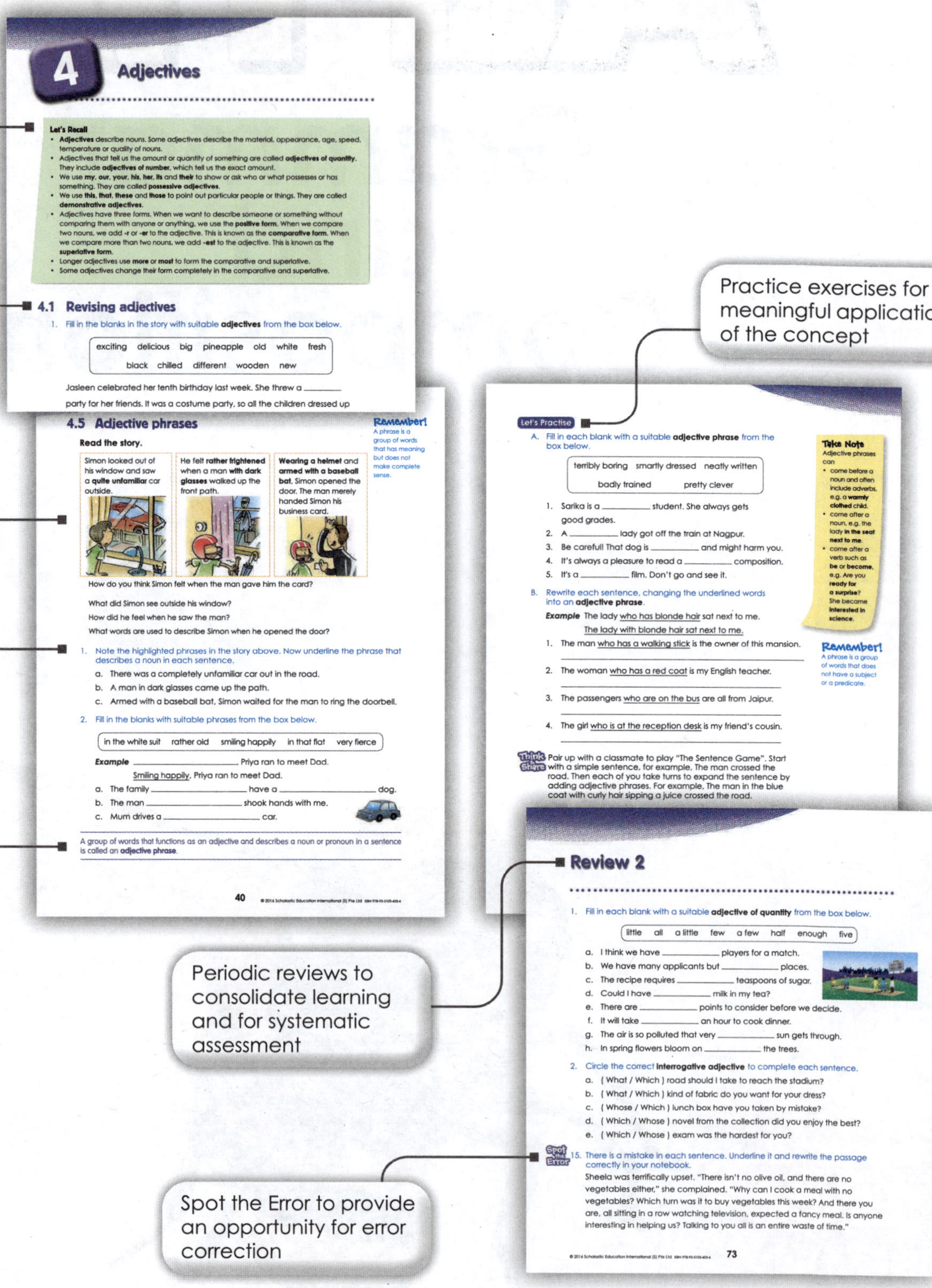

4 Adjectives

Let's Recall
- Adjectives describe nouns. Some adjectives describe the material, appearance, age, speed, temperature or quality of nouns.
- Adjectives that tell us the amount or quantity of something are called adjectives of quantity. They include adjectives of number, which tell us the exact amount.
- We use my, our, your, his, her, its and their to show or ask who or what possesses or has something. They are called possessive adjectives.
- We use this, that, these and those to point out particular people or things. They are called demonstrative adjectives.
- Adjectives have three forms. When we want to describe someone or something without comparing them with anyone or anything, we use the positive form. When we compare two nouns, we add -r or -er to the adjective. This is known as the comparative form. When we compare more than two nouns, we add -est to the adjective. This is known as the superlative form.
- Longer adjectives use more or most to form the comparative and superlative.
- Some adjectives change their form completely in the comparative and superlative.

4.1 Revising adjectives

1. Fill in the blanks in the story with suitable adjectives from the box below.

exciting delicious big pineapple old white fresh black chilled different wooden new

Jasleen celebrated her tenth birthday last week. She threw a ________ party for her friends. It was a costume party, so all the children dressed up

4.5 Adjective phrases

Read the story.

Simon looked out of his window and saw a quite unfamiliar car outside.

He felt rather frightened when a man with dark glasses walked up the front path.

Wearing a helmet and armed with a baseball bat, Simon opened the door. The man merely handed Simon his business card.

Remember! A phrase is a group of words that has meaning but does not make complete sense.

How do you think Simon felt when the man gave him the card?

What did Simon see outside his window?

How did he feel when he saw the man?

What words are used to describe Simon when he opened the door?

1. Note the highlighted phrases in the story above. Now underline the phrase that describes a noun in each sentence.
   a. There was a completely unfamiliar car out in the road.
   b. A man in dark glasses came up the path.
   c. Armed with a baseball bat, Simon waited for the man to ring the doorbell.
2. Fill in the blanks with suitable phrases from the box below.

in the white suit rather old smiling happily in that flat very fierce

Example ________ Priya ran to meet Dad.
Smiling happily, Priya ran to meet Dad.
   a. The family ________ have a ________ dog.
   b. The man ________ shook hands with me.
   c. Mum drives a ________ car.

A group of words that functions as an adjective and describes a noun or pronoun in a sentence is called an adjective phrase.

40

Let's Practise

A. Fill in each blank with a suitable adjective phrase from the box below.

terribly boring smartly dressed neatly written badly trained pretty clever

1. Sarika is a ________ student. She always gets good grades.
2. A ________ lady got off the train at Nagpur.
3. Be careful! That dog is ________ and might harm you.
4. It's always a pleasure to read a ________ composition.
5. It's a ________ film. Don't go and see it.

B. Rewrite each sentence, changing the underlined words into an adjective phrase.

Example The lady who has blonde hair sat next to me.
The lady with blonde hair sat next to me.
1. The man who has a walking stick is the owner of this mansion.
2. The woman who has a red coat is my English teacher.
3. The passengers who are on the bus are all from Jaipur.
4. The girl who is at the reception desk is my friend's cousin.

Take Note Adjective phrases can
- come before a noun and often include adverbs, e.g. a warmly clothed child.
- come after a noun, e.g. the lady in the seat next to me.
- come after a verb such as be or become, e.g. Are you ready for a surprise? She became interested in science.

Remember! A phrase is a group of words that does not have a subject or a predicate.

Think & Share Pair up with a classmate to play "The Sentence Game". Start with a simple sentence, for example, The man crossed the road. Then each of you take turns to expand the sentence by adding adjective phrases. For example, The man in the blue coat with curly hair sipping a juice crossed the road.

Review 2

1. Fill in each blank with a suitable adjective of quantity from the box below.

little all a little few a few half enough five

   a. I think we have ________ players for a match.
   b. We have many applicants but ________ places.
   c. The recipe requires ________ teaspoons of sugar.
   d. Could I have ________ milk in my tea?
   e. There are ________ points to consider before we decide.
   f. It will take ________ an hour to cook dinner.
   g. The air is so polluted that very ________ sun gets through.
   h. In spring flowers bloom on ________ the trees.
2. Circle the correct interrogative adjective to complete each sentence.
   a. (What / Which) road should I take to reach the stadium?
   b. (What / Which) kind of fabric do you want for your dress?
   c. (Whose / Which) lunch box have you taken by mistake?
   d. (Which / Whose) novel from the collection did you enjoy the best?
   e. (Which / Whose) exam was the hardest for you?

Spot the Error 15. There is a mistake in each sentence. Underline it and rewrite the passage correctly in your notebook.
Sheela was terrifically upset. "There isn't no olive oil, and there are no vegetables either," she complained. "Why can I cook a meal with no vegetables? Which turn was it to buy vegetables this week? And there you are, all sitting in a row watching television, expected a fancy meal. Is anyone interesting in helping us? Talking to you all is an entire waste of time."

73

- **Take Note** provides additional tips and exceptions to rules.
- **Think & Share** activities allow opportunity for collaborative learning.
- **Remember** enhances the understanding of the concept being taught in the unit.

 ISBN 978-93-5103-603-6

Graded exercises develop key comprehension and critical thinking skills

Scaffolded exercises to develop key writing skills across varied genres and topics

Vocabulary building through engaging exercises

 ISBN 978-93-5103-603-6

Contents

 ISBN 978-93-5103-603-6

8 Conjunctions

9 Sentences

10 Questions

11 Punctuation

12 Comprehension

13 Composition

 ISBN 978-93-5103-603-6

1 Nouns

Let's Recall

- **Common nouns** are names for people, places, animals and things. **Proper nouns** are names for particular people, places, animals and things.
- Nouns are either **singular** (one) or **plural** (more than one). Some nouns have plural forms that are quite different from the singular form. These are called **irregular plurals**.
- **Countable nouns** are names for things that can be counted. **Uncountable nouns** are names for things that cannot be counted.
- **Collective nouns** are names for groups of people, animals or things.
- **Masculine nouns** refer to males and **feminine nouns** to females. **Common-gender nouns** refer to both males and females. **Neuter nouns** refer to places and non-living things.
- We add **'s** to singular nouns to show possession. We do this even if the noun or proper name ends in **-s**. With plural nouns ending in **-s** we add only the apostrophe ('). With plurals that don't end in **-s** we add **'s**. This is called the **possessive** form of the **noun**.
- **Concrete nouns** are names for things that we can see or touch. **Abstract nouns** are names for things that we cannot see or touch.
- **Compound nouns** are nouns made up of two or sometimes three words.

1.1 Revising nouns

1. Match the **proper nouns** with the **common nouns**.

a. Mumbai •	• i. a building
b. Kanchenjunga •	• ii. a monument
c. Burj Khalifa •	• iii. a leader
d. the Qutb Minar •	• iv. a book
e. Antarctica •	• v. a country
f. *The Little Prince* •	• vi. a mountain
g. Jawaharlal Nehru •	• vii. a continent
h. Myanmar •	• viii. a city

2. Circle the **proper nouns** and underline the **common nouns**. Then rewrite each sentence using capital letters where needed.

   a. ravi and his family visited egypt and saw the pyramids.

   ____

   b. the statue of liberty stands at the entrance to the harbour in new york.

   ____

 ISBN 978-93-5103-603-6

c. sir stamford raffles realised that singapore could become a centre of trade.

____

d. My favourite book is matilda by roald dahl.

____

e. hari and shashi go to a school in richmond town.

____

3. Circle the **singular nouns** and underline the **plural nouns** in the sentences below.

a. When babies get their first teeth, they chew every object they can pick up.
b. My sister is allergic to shellfish.
c. Tina's wet feet left a trail of footprints from the bathroom to the bedroom.
d. The police set up cameras to catch speeding drivers.
e. An early jet was one of the aircraft we saw in the display.
f. Jo's children often pay a visit to their grandparents in Pune.
g. Many years ago dinosaurs used to roam over this plain.
h. Farmers keep sheepdogs to guard their sheep.

4. Fill in the blanks in the story with the correct **plural** form of the **nouns** given in the brackets.

Asha, Sid and I were walking in the hills when a storm broke, the worst we had ever seen in our ________ (life). The ________ (branch) of the ________ (tree) started waving about violently, and the ________ (leaf) shook. We stopped to put on our ________ (jersey) and ________ (raincoat) as ________ (flurry) of rain blew towards us. The wind grew very violent as we struggled on, and seemed to be twisting about, like one of those ________ (tornado) we had seen in films. Then suddenly there was a flash of lightning, and then more ________ (flash). The ________ (echo) of the thunder resounded all through the surrounding hills and ________ (valley). We looked for shelter, but there were only some little ________ (bush) on the hillside. After a while the storm rolled away and we walked home, relieved at last to see the familiar red ________ (roof) of the village where we were staying.

 ISBN 978-93-5103-603-6

5. Fill in each blank with the correct form of **be**, **have** or **do** to match the **noun** in the sentence.

Remember!
The verbs **is**, **am**, **are**, **was** and **were** are forms of the verb **be**.

a. Look! My jeans __________ shrunk in the wash!
b. That new pair of glasses __________ not suit you.
c. The blue scissors __________ very sharp.
d. Here __________ a clean pair of shorts for you.
e. My swimming goggles __________ misting up.
f. A pair of chopsticks __________ enclosed in the pack.
g. How __________ the binoculars work?
h. Where __________ my black pair of trousers?

6. Circle the **countable nouns** and underline the **uncountable nouns**. Then rewrite each sentence correctly, using **a** or **an** before the countable nouns.

a. Could I have cup of coffee with milk and sugar?

____

b. Much knowledge can be gained by consulting encyclopaedia.

____

c. Sally was wearing dress made of silk.

____

d. You can't ride bicycle in deep mud.

____

e. Would you like orange?

____

f. Bindya made toy out of recycled paper.

____

7. Fill in the blanks with **some** or **any**.

Remember!
- We use **a** or **an** before countable nouns.
- We use **some** or **any** before uncountable nouns.

a. We need __________ bread and __________ butter.
b. Fred never takes __________ exercise.
c. I don't want __________ toast, but I'd like __________ cornflakes.
d. If there's __________ trouble, Dad usually has __________ good advice.
e. I helped myself to __________ ice cream.
f. I need __________ information about this unusual bird.
g. Don't you want __________ soup today?
h. I need __________ string and a pair of scissors.

 ISBN 978-93-5103-603-6

8. Fill in each blank with the correct word from the box below to match the **uncountable noun**.

loaf	slice	roll	carton	drop	bar	grain
blade	stick	block	pane	sheet		

a. a ________ of paper

b. a ________ of ice

c. a ________ of cheese

d. a ________ of grass

e. a ________ of chocolate

f. a ________ of chalk

g. a ________ of glass

h. a ________ of bread

i. a ________ of toilet paper

j. a ________ of rice

k. a ________ of juice

l. a ________ of blood

9. Complete the sentences with the help of the pictures, using suitable **collective nouns** from the box below.

string of	set of	range of	swarm of	regiment of
wad of	album of	anthology of		

a. In the distance we could see a ____________________.

b.  Tarun took out a ____________________ to pay the taxi driver.

c. After a long search Shirin found her ____________________ at the back of a drawer.

d.  We cheered as each ____________________ marched smartly down Rajpath during the Republic Day parade.

e. Always keep a ____________________ in your car. 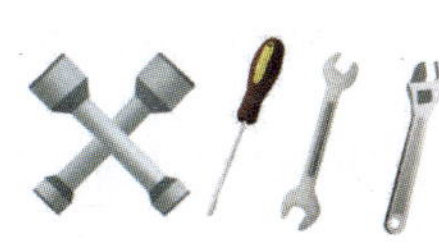

f.  A ____________________ crawled over the fallen leaves in the garden.

g. Hasan showed me an ____________________ taken on his trip to Nepal.

h. 

Shubha's aunt gave her an ____________________ by Rabindranath Tagore for her birthday.

 ISBN 978-93-5103-603-6

10. Circle the correct verb to match the **collective noun** in each sentence.

Remember!
We use a singular verb with a collective noun if we are thinking of the group as a whole. We use a plural verb with a collective noun if we are thinking of the individual people or things in the group.

a. The audience (was / were) taking their seats.

b. Most nights the audience (consists / consist) mainly of women.

c. The orchestra (is / are) all waiting for the conductor to appear.

d. The orchestra (has / have) included some charity concerts in its programme.

e. The council (is / are) made up of a chairman, a secretary and ten members.

f. The council (is / are) discussing the issue of rubbish collection.

g. My family (comes / come) from Orissa.

h. My family always (gathers / gather) for a get-together in the summer.

11. Write **M** for masculine, **F** for feminine, **N** for neuter or **CG** for common-gender nouns in the brackets in the story below.

Zubaida and her friends [ ] were sitting in a café [ ] waiting for someone to bring them the menu [ ]. They were discussing the film [ ] they had seen the night [ ] before. It was an old film called *Mandy*. It was about a five-year-old girl [ ] who was completely deaf and could not speak. Her dad [ ] wanted to keep his daughter [ ] safe in the house [ ] and not let her play with other children [ ]. Her mum [ ] wanted her to learn to lip-read and speak so that she could be like everyone else. She found Mandy a teacher [ ], who taught Mandy to speak by getting her to put her lips [ ] against a balloon [ ] when she was screaming, so that she could feel the vibration [ ] of her own voice [ ]. Zubaida and her companions [ ] thought it was a wonderful story [ ]. Then along came the waiter [ ] and took their order [ ], and they enjoyed their drinks [ ] and cakes [ ].

12. Replace the underlined masculine or feminine noun in each sentence with a **common-gender noun**. Write it in the blank.

Example Joanna wanted to be a ballerina. dancer

a. I spoke to the woman behind me. ________

b. Deepak and Shruti were delighted when their son was born. ________

 ISBN 978-93-5103-603-6

c. The air hostess brought me some water. ________

d. Your mum and dad are invited to the school concert. ________

e. The fire was tackled by a team of firemen. ________

f. A policeman came round to ask some questions. ________

g. "Girls and boys, please take your seats," said the teacher. ________

h. Asha was thrilled to see her grandfather and grandmother. ________

13. Fill in each blank with the **possessive** form of the **noun** given in the brackets.

Remember!
If two nouns joined by **and** are both the owners of something, we add **'s** after the second noun to show belonging.

a. After leaving university, Isha went back to live at her ____________ house. (parents)

b. Anna and ____________ cat was found at last. (Denis)

c. I'm shocked at some ____________ behaviour. (people)

d. Vijay shook his ____________ hand politely as he left. (hostess)

e. I've been invited to the ____________ flat for dinner. (Johnsons)

f. The Greek ____________ home was on Mount Olympus. (goddesses)

g. Do you have Mrs ____________ address? (Das)

h. Miss Reddy took all her ____________ test papers home with her to mark. (pupils)

i. The dog could hear his ____________ voice calling him. (mistress)

j. We volunteered to help build a ____________ playground. (children)

14. Fill in each blank with the **possessive** form of a **noun** from the box below.

Sheela	cat	parents	baby	principal	Mum	George

Example If George has Peter's exercise book, Peter must have George's.

a. Helping children with their homework isn't the teachers' job. It's the ____________.

b. The dog's feeding bowl is over there and the ____________ is here.

c. If this book is not yours, then it must be ____________.

d. Dad's passport has been found, but where is ____________?

e. This is the school secretary's room. The ____________ is along the corridor.

f. This is Anju's dinner. Where is the ____________ milk?

Take Note
We can use the possessive form without a noun following it, e.g. This isn't my scarf. It's **Susan's**.

 ISBN 978-93-5103-603-6

15. Circle the **concrete nouns** and underline the **abstract nouns** in the story below.

On every day except Friday, the pupils at Silverbridge School have to wear their uniforms. On Friday, for fun, everyone is allowed to wear anything they like. So, when the children sit down at their desks, the classrooms have a much brighter and more colourful look than they do on other mornings. Khushi always has trouble deciding what to wear. Should she wear her blue sweater with her corduroy trousers, or her purple top with her pink leggings? When she is dressed, she gets her coat and bag, and walks to the gates of the school.

16. Complete the tables with **abstract nouns**. Choose a suitable ending from the box below to add to each verb or adjective.

-ance -ty -ence -ion -ity -ment -ness -hood -y

	Adjective	Abstract noun
Example	bold	boldness
a.	dark	
b.	equal	
c.	false	
d.	helpful	
e.	honest	
f.	jealous	
g.	likely	
h.	loyal	
i.	mad	
j.	modest	
k.	novel	
l.	popular	
m.	stupid	
n.	weak	

	Verb	Abstract noun
Example	act	action
a.	amaze	
b.	annoy	
c.	attend	
d.	direct	
e.	discuss	
f.	exist	
g.	instruct	
h.	manage	
i.	move	
j.	perform	
k.	prefer	
l.	punish	
m.	refer	
n.	subtract	

17. Fill in each blank with an **abstract noun** formed from the word given in the brackets.

a. Hari spent his ______________ in Sri Lanka. (boy)

b. The people in this city are known for their ______________. (friendly)

 ISBN 978-93-5103-603-6

c. Don't change your plans now. It will just cause ______________. (confuse)

d. You will need travel ______________ if you go abroad. (insure)

e. The New Democratic Party won the election with a huge ______________. (major)

f. Sam and Mary were having an ______________ about money. (argue)

18. Underline the **compound noun** in each sentence.

Example You are welcome to test our range of beauty products.

a. There was a pile of magazines in the waiting room.

b. Put the waste into this recycling bin.

c. A concrete-mixer blocked the road ahead.

d. We have a dancing lesson at three o'clock.

e. It just needs common sense to answer these questions.

f. Dental hygiene is very important for good health.

g. The lorry-driver backed into a wall.

h. Dad bought a newspaper from the shop.

i. I left my magnifying glass in the study.

j. All my favourite books are on this bookshelf.

19. Fill in each blank with a suitable **compound noun** from the box below.

beauty cream	living room	superstar	
doll's house	runner-up	hair-curlers	flowerpot
washing machine	air-conditioner	parking light	

a. Turn on the ______________. It's very hot.

b. We need some new furniture for the ______________.

c. Mrs Goel wears ______________ at night.

d. Vinita got a ______________ on her birthday.

e. The cat is sleeping near the ______________.

f. Dad left the ______________ on again.

g. The ______________ was given a silver medal.

h. This new ______________ does not suit me at all.

i. Ameya's family bought a new ______________ last week.

j. Sumeet is going to watch a film starring her favourite ______________.

 ISBN 978-93-5103-603-6

1.2 Noun phrases

Remember!
A group of words that has meaning but does not make complete sense is called a phrase.

Read the story.

John Harris landed **the passenger aircraft** safely at the airport.

The flight crew entered **the terminal building**. They were followed by **the first passengers**.

John got **a warm welcome** from **his family**.

What did John get for his family? Do you think they were happy to get them?

What did John land?

Who entered the terminal building?

What did John get from his family?

1. Fill in each blank with a suitable phrase from the story above.
   a. After a long flight, the pilot landed ____________________ at Manston Airport.
   b. Mr and Mrs Dawson were ____________________ to get off the plane.
   c. The winning team got ____________________ when they reached home.

2. Complete each sentence with a suitable phrase from the box below. Circle the noun in the phrase.

some exciting news	chilled watermelon	a long journey
many different languages	their new neighbour	

   a. Lewis Carroll's books have been translated into ____________________.
   b. I like to have ____________________ on a hot summer day.
   c. The Batras invited ____________________ to their Diwali party.
   d. After ____________________, they finally reached the fort.
   e. Ritika has ____________________ for us!

A phrase that acts like a noun in a sentence is called a **noun phrase**.

 ISBN 978-93-5103-603-6

Let's Practise

A. Read the story and answer each question below with a **noun phrase**.

Today we helped the class teacher to decorate the Christmas tree. First we put it into a wooden tub, and packed crumpled newspaper round its thick trunk. We arranged coloured lights over the green branches. In the box of decorations we found little silver glass balls to hang on them. Our Christmas tree was a lovely sight.

Example Whom did the children help? the class teacher

1. What did they decorate? ______________________
2. What did they put it into? ______________________
3. What did they pack round it?______________________
4. What did they arrange over the branches? ______________
5. What did they hang on the branches? ______________
6. What was a lovely sight? ______________________

Take Note
Just like a noun, a noun phrase can be the subject or object of a verb, e.g. Ravi enjoys **playing football** (object of the verb). A noun phrase can also be the object of a preposition, e.g. Rima made a pie with **lots of cheese** (object of the preposition).

B. Look at the picture. Then answer each question with a **noun phrase**.

Take Note
A noun phrase is often formed by adding articles or adjectives to the noun.

1. What is curled up on the armchair? ______________
2. What is on the table? ______________
3. What can you see on each side of the window? ______________
4. What is hanging on the wall? ______________

Think & Share Pair up with a classmate. Make a list of ten nouns each. Think of a noun phrase for each noun and share the list with your partner.

 ISBN 978-93-5103-603-6

2 Pronouns

Let's Recall

- **Pronouns** are words that take the place of nouns in a sentence.
- **I, we, you, he, she, it, they, me, us, him, her** and **them** are called **personal pronouns.**
- **I, me, we** and **us** refer to the person or people speaking. They are called **first-person pronouns**. **You** refers to the person or people spoken to. This is the **second-person pronoun. He, she, it, they, him, her** and **them** refer to the person, people or things that we are speaking about. They are called **third-person pronouns.**
- **Mine, yours, his, hers, ours** and **theirs** are pronouns that show possession. They are called **possessive pronouns.**

2.1 Revising pronouns

1. Fill in each blank with a **personal pronoun**.

   a. I want ______ all to take these letters home and give ______ to your parents.

   b. Where's Sally? Oh, there ______ is. I didn't see ______ standing there.

   c. Why are ______ crying? Tell ______ what is wrong.

   d. Hello, Mrs Shetty! May ______ carry that bag for ______?

   e. George was in the park yesterday. ______ had his dog with ______.

   f. Hina's parents take their pet parrot with ______ wherever ______ go.

2. Circle the correct **possessive pronoun** to complete each sentence.

   a. Parul's exam results arrived today, but I haven't received (hers / mine).

   b. Mala is using my dancing shoes while (mine / hers) are being repaired.

   c. No, that isn't Joe's bike. (His / Theirs) has thicker tyres.

   d. It's difficult to park a car here, so we didn't bring (yours / ours) today.

3. Fill in each blank with a **personal** or **possessive pronoun**.

   a. My mobile phone isn't working. May ______ borrow ______, James?

   b. This coat looks like Sheela's, but ______ says ______ isn't ______.

   c. Hari, if your bicycle is damaged, ______ can use ______.

   d. Ajay says ______ forgot to take his mobile-charger with ______.

   e. Our garden isn't as large as the Kumars', but ______ is prettier than ______.

 ISBN 978-93-5103-603-6

2.2 Reflexive pronouns

Remember!
The subject is the naming part of a sentence. It can be a noun, pronoun or group of words that tells us what the sentence is about.

Read the story.

We had organised a surprise party for Mum. When Mum let **herself** in, everyone cheered!

The guests were invited to help **themselves** to all the delicious food.

"Are you enjoying **yourself**?" asked Nina. "Oh yes! I've never enjoyed **myself** as much as this!" replied Mum.

What was the surprise party for? How can you tell?

How did Mum get into the house?

What were the guests invited to do?

What did Nina ask Mum?

1. Note the highlighted pronouns in the story above. Now fill in the blanks with them.

   Dad told the guests to hide ______ behind the door as Mum walked in. Sue hid ______ behind the table.

   "I'll hide ______ behind this chair," whispered Anna.

   When Mum entered, everyone jumped out and yelled "Happy birthday!"

   "Help ______ to the food!" Dad told each of the guests.

2. Underline the subject in each of the sentences below. Circle the pronoun that refers to it.

   a. Anna hid herself behind a chair.
   b. Did you enjoy yourselves?
   c. Dad cut himself with a sharp knife.
   d. I taught myself to swim.
   e. The muddy dog licked itself clean.
   f. We dressed ourselves quickly.

The singular pronouns **myself**, **yourself**, **himself**, **herself** and **itself** and the plural pronouns **ourselves**, **yourselves** and **themselves** are called **reflexive pronouns**. They refer to the person, animal or thing that is the subject of the verb.

 ISBN 978-93-5103-603-6

Let's Practise

A. Fill in each blank with a **reflexive pronoun**.

1. Many of you can already express ________________ well in English.
2. Mahika blamed ________________ for the accident.
3. Go on, treat ________________ to this delicious cake, Sania!
4. Why don't we all introduce ________________?
5. Baby Paul can feed ________________ already.
6. Kumar and Venu tired ________________ out swimming across the river.
7. The elephant sprayed water all over ________________ with its trunk.
8. I need time to organise ________________ in the morning.
9. Can you and Peter entertain ________________ while I'm out?
10. Hema and I booked ________________ into the best hotel.
11. Spies have to train ________________ to watch without being noticed.
12. Jamila woke up to find ________________ in hospital.

B. Fill in each blank with a **preposition** from the top box and a **reflexive pronoun** from the lower box.

to	by	with	of	on	for	after	at

myself	yourself	himself	herself	itself
ourselves	yourselves	themselves		

1. Don't buy my ticket. I'll pay ________________.
2. When you grow up, Danny, you'll have to look ________________.
3. Tushar glanced ________________ in the mirror.
4. Children, you must consider other people instead of always thinking ________________.
5. We were cross ________________ for losing our way.
6. Old people sometimes talk ________________.
7. The wild cat depends ________________ and finds food by hunting.
8. Gina was sitting all ________________ in the classroom.

Take Note
A reflexive pronoun can be used after a preposition, e.g. You worry **about yourself** too much. They had to cook **for themselves**.

Think & Share Make three columns on a sheet. List five nouns (people and animals) and five personal pronouns in column 1 and all the reflexive pronouns in column 2. Stick pictures of food and drink in column 3. Take turns to make funny sentences using one item from each column, for example, The cat makes itself a cup of tea.

 ISBN 978-93-5103-603-6

2.3 Emphasising pronouns

Read the story.

Mum was making a pie. Tim complained that no one asked him what he **himself** wanted.

Jane had been helping Mum while Mum **herself** was busy.

"Tim, here is your favourite salad," said Jane. "I made it **myself**."

Do you think Tim was pleased to get the salad? Why do you think so?

Did Tim like pies? How do you know?

Why did Jane help Mum?

What did Jane tell Tim?

1. Note the highlighted pronouns in the story above. Now fill in each blank with a suitable pronoun that puts emphasis on the underlined noun(s) or pronoun.

   a. Tim wanted to choose his food ______________.

   b. Mum and Jane liked pies ______________, even if Tim didn't.

   c. Jane made the salad ______________.

   d. "I prefer pies ______________," said Jane.

2. Circle the pronoun that puts emphasis on the underlined noun or pronoun.

   a. I know the car was locked because I locked it myself.

   b. If you want something done, do it yourself.

   c. Harry was certainly at the party. We saw him ourselves.

   d. Don't help Shashi with her homework. She must do it herself.

   e. The book itself was old and dirty, but the story inside was exciting.

   f. The volunteers will come round themselves to collect donations for the flood-affected people.

   g. Girls, I've no time to iron your clothes. Please iron them yourselves.

Reflexive pronouns are sometimes used to emphasise a noun or pronoun. When they are used in this way, they are called **emphasising pronouns**.

 ISBN 978-93-5103-603-6

Let's Practise

A. Look at the underlined pronoun in each sentence. In the brackets, write **R** for reflexive or **E** for emphasising.

1. Vijay drove himself to the meeting. [ ]
2. We didn't approve of the play ourselves. [ ]
3. Please don't upset yourself over nothing. [ ]
4. I've seen myself what damage an oil leak can do. [ ]
5. Oh, the phone's ringing. Could you see yourselves out? [ ]
6. The witch changed herself into a frog. [ ]
7. This is the right answer. Check it yourself. [ ]
8. They know themselves that what they did was wrong. [ ]

Take Note
An emphasising pronoun can be removed from the sentence without affecting its basic meaning. A reflexive pronoun is essential to the meaning of the sentence.

B. Rewrite each sentence, adding an **emphasising pronoun** for the underlined noun or pronoun.

1. Can you copy those files, or shall I help you?
___
2. I want to speak to the boss and to no one else.
___
3. The palace is closed to visitors, but you can walk in the grounds.
___

4. Mr and Mrs Rao, have you ever done any rock climbing?
___
5. It looks an easy golf course, but the golfers find it difficult.
___
6. We enjoyed the play, and we heard that the author was in the audience.
___
7. I realised that I'd made a bad mistake.
___
8. We don't care for football. We prefer tennis.
___

9. Has Kate ever skated?
___
10. I don't know Mona, but I know her friends.
___

 ISBN 978-93-5103-603-6

2.4 Interrogative pronouns

Read the story.

Carla was doing a history project. "Mum, **who** was Ashoka?" she asked. "Ashoka was a great king," Mum replied.

"**What** do you want to know about him ?" asked Mum, reaching for her encyclopaedia.

"**Whom** did he rule over?" asked Carla. "He ruled over the people of India," said Mum.

What else do you think Carla needs to know for her project?

What was Carla's first question?

What did Mum ask Carla?

What else did Carla want to know?

1. Fill in each blank with a suitable pronoun from the story above.

   a. ________ was King Ashoka?

   b. ________ did he rule over?

   c. ________ did Carla want to know?

   d. ________ was able to help her?

2. Write a question for each sentence. Begin with **who**, **whose**, **whom**, **what** or **which**.

   Example The suitcase with the blue tag is mine.

   Which is your suitcase?

   a. Shobha is knocking at the door.

   ____

   b. This will be the best option.

   ____

   c. The doctor told me to take a week's rest.

   ____

   d. This pen is my teacher's.

   ____

The pronouns **who**, **whose**, **whom**, **what** or **which** are used to ask questions. They are called **interrogative pronouns**.

 ISBN 978-93-5103-603-6

Let's Practise

A. Fill in each blank with an **interrogative pronoun**. In the brackets, write **S** if it is singular or **P** if it is plural.

Example Over whom did Ashoka reign? [P]

1. ______ is captain of the team? [ ]
2. ______ are these laptops? [ ]
3. ______ of the players have been chosen for the team? [ ]
4. ______ keeps the Earth warm? [ ]
5. ______ is your badminton racquet? [ ]

Take Note
Interrogative pronouns are question words used on their own to ask for a person or thing to be identified. The answer is a noun or a pronoun.

B. Fill in each blank with **who** or **whom**.

1. To ______ shall I address the letter?
2. ______ wants to come with me?
3. ______ are you taking to the flower show?
4. ______ can be trusted with the message?
5. From ______ is the message?

C. Circle the correct **interrogative pronoun** to complete each sentence.

1. (Who / Whom) wants to come with me to the park?
2. To (who / whom) shall I send my application?
3. (Whom / Whose) is the best drawing in the competition?
4. Somebody's mobile phone started ringing during the concert. Do you know (who / whose) it was?
5. Have you decided (what / whom) you want to be when you grow up?
6. (Which / What) would you prefer, an ice cream or a juice?
7. Jane and Ruth are the same age, but (who / which) of them is the taller?
8. Those flowers are lilies, but do you know (which / what) these are?

Take Note
- Interrogative pronouns can be singular or plural, e.g. **Whose is** this coat? (singular). **Whose are** all these coats? (plural).
- We use **who** if the pronoun is the subject of the verb (**Who** said that?), and **who** or **whom** if it is the object of the verb (**Who/Whom** do you mean?). We must use **whom** if the pronoun follows a preposition, e.g. About **whom** was Carla finding out?

Think & Share Play a game of twenty questions with your partner. Think of a famous personality and ask your partner to guess their identity by asking questions using interrogative pronouns, for example, **Who** was she? **What** was she famous for?

 ISBN 978-93-5103-603-6

3 Articles

Let's Recall

- The words **a**, **an** and **the** are called **articles**. They are used before nouns.
- We use **a** or **an** before a noun when we don't mean a particular one. We use **an** before a noun beginning with a vowel.
- We use **the** when we mean a particular noun.
- **A** and **an** are **indefinite articles. The** is a **definite article**.
- Some nouns can be used without an article.

3.1 Revising articles

1. Fill in the blanks in the story with a suitable **article**. Write (**0**) in the blank if an article is not required.

Tom had moved back home recently from ______ Hong Kong to live with his family in ______ United States. He usually went to work by ______ car, but his car had broken down that morning. He decided to stay at ______ home and work. There was ______ computer in ______ sitting room for ______ use of all ______ family. Tom had ______ task to do on it, but when he sat down at ______ desk he found that its surface was all covered with ______ crumbs, just as if someone had been eating ______ biscuit, and ______ biscuit had broken all over ______ desk. Tom sighed and began cleaning ______ desk.

Remember!

- We use **a** or **an** before countable nouns when we mention them for the first time. We use **the** when we mention them again.
- We don't use an article before uncountable nouns or plural nouns when we mention them for the first time. We use **the** when we mention them again.

2. Rewrite each sentence adding **a**, **an** or **the** wherever necessary.

   a. I had orange and apple for breakfast, along with bowl of cornflakes, but I'm still hungry!

   ____

   b. Hina has made decision to study music at college in Belgium.

   ____

   c. I went into town by bus to buy outfit for school dance.

   ____

   d. George pulled back bedclothes and got into bed.

   ____

 ISBN 978-93-5103-603-6

3.2 More uses of the definite article

Read the story.

Jack was choosing a calculator. "Which is **the best** one for me?" he wondered.

The assistant showed him two calculators. **The first** was **the larger** and **the more useful**. But Jack quite liked **the second**, **smaller** one.

In the end he decided on **the larger** one, although it was **the most expensive** in the case.

Do you think Jack made the right decision? Why do you think so?

What did Jack wonder while choosing a calculator?

What were the calculators like?

Which calculator did Jack finally decide to buy?

1. Note how **the** is used in the story above. In the brackets, write **C** for the correct or **I** for the incorrect use of the definite article

   a. This calculator is the better than that one. [ ]

   b. Jack liked the smaller one. [ ]

   c. Jack decided to buy the larger and the most expensive calculator. [ ]

2. Rewrite each sentence using **the** where needed.

   a. Summer is second season of the year.

   ____

   b. We climbed to the summit of highest hill.

   ____

   c. Natalie was taller of the twins.

   ____

   d. Third day of our holiday was hottest.

   ____

Remember!

- **The** is used before things if there is only one, e.g. **the** sun.
- **The** is used before environmental things, e.g. **the** weather.
- **The** is used before a thing or person if there is only one we could mean, e.g. **the** door.

The definite article **the** is often used with comparatives and superlatives. **The** is also used with number words that show the order of nouns.

 ISBN 978-93-5103-603-6

Let's Practise

A. Circle the correct option to complete each sentence.

1. What is (the saddest / a sad) moment in the story?
2. Wednesday is (fourth / the fourth) day of the week.
3. That was (the loudest / a loud) thunderstorm of the entire summer.
4. Nidhi gave (the sweeter / sweeter) mango to her sister.
5. In India, Children's Day is celebrated on (fourteenth / the fourteenth) of November every year.
6. Mukul pointed to (brightest / the brightest) star in the sky.
7. April Fool's Day is (the first / first) of April.
8. Anisha is (the older / older) of the two children.
9. Christmas Day is always on (the twenty-fifth / twenty-fifth) of December.
10. Which is (largest / the largest) mammal?

Take Note

- You use **the** when you compare two people or things without using **than**, e.g. **The smaller** size fits me fine.
- You use **the** when you refer to something or someone unique, e.g. Mohit is **the best** runner. Sheila was **the only** person left behind.

B. Rewrite each sentence adding **the** wherever necessary.

1. This is fourth time computer has crashed today.

   ____

2. Simran packed her books in larger suitcase.

   ____

3. This is tallest tree in park.

   ____

4. On fifth of March we travel by plane to Paris.

   ____

5. Little Abu was only one who got last question right.

   ____

6. Rosie thought of best answer to third question.

   ____

7. Sally is prettiest of three sisters, but Sophie is most intelligent.

   ____

8. Tommy was friendliest dog in pound.

   ____

 ISBN 978-93-5103-603-6

Review 1

1. Expand each underlined noun into a **noun phrase** using a group of words from the box below. Rewrite the sentence and underline the complete noun phrase.

at the reception desk	some necessary	tall uniformed	with a ponytail
valuable gold	all your hand	very kind, thoughtful	

Example Jenny was wearing a ring.

Jenny was wearing a valuable gold ring.

a. I opened the door to a police officer.

____

b. We must buy provisions for our holiday.

____

c. The lady asked us to wait.

____

d. Payal was talking to a girl.

____

e. Please take luggage with you when you leave the plane.

____

f. Thank you so much for the present.

____

2. Underline the **noun phrases** in the story.

It was a bright, sunny morning. David walked down to the big broad river holding his father's hand. He was carrying a long thin fishing rod, given to him for his seventh birthday. Dad was carrying a large lunchbox in which there were cheese sandwiches and a chocolate cake to eat later. When they reached the grassy riverbank, Dad spread out a thick tartan rug for them to sit on. Dad fitted his own fishing rod together and showed David how to cast his fishing line into the deep water. David copied Dad and, by a piece of extraordinary luck, managed to hook a big fish at his very first attempt. Dad helped David to land his amazing catch.

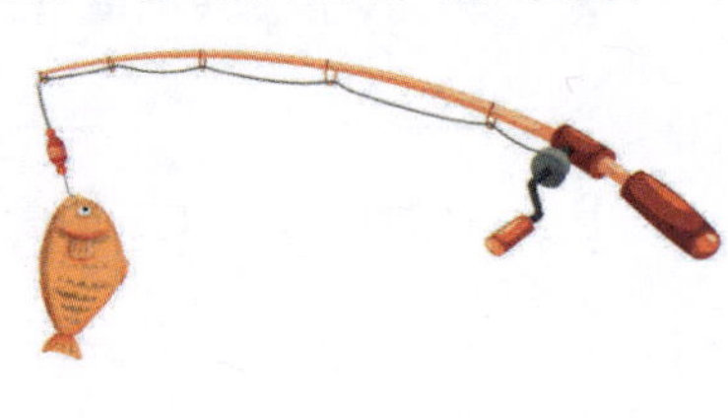

 ISBN 978-93-5103-603-6

3. Fill in each blank with a suitable **reflexive pronoun**.

a. I congratulated ________ on getting the answer right.
b. Please help ________ to the food, everyone.
c. Hotel guests served ________ from the array of breakfast dishes.
d. Oh, Shilpa, did you hurt ________?
e. The wizard changed ________ into a snake.
f. The Art teacher told us to draw ________.
g. Kiran locked ________ into her bedroom.
h. To our shock, we found a tiger sunning ________ on our veranda.

4. Circle the **reflexive pronoun** in each sentence. Underline the subject it refers to.

a. I must get a new laptop for myself.
b. Mohit blamed himself for the accident.
c. I hope you are ashamed of yourselves.
d. The children now walk to school by themselves.
e. Consider yourself lucky that you can actually attend school.
f. Mum looked at herself in the mirror.
g. Suraj hadn't had time to tidy himself up.
h. Harry and I had the restaurant all to ourselves.

5. Look at the underlined **pronoun** in each sentence. Tick the correct box to indicate if it is **reflexive** or **emphasising**.

	Reflexive	Emphasising
a. You should have answered the phone yourself.	☐	☐
b. I can't help wondering myself if it's true.	☐	☐
c. Joe forced himself to apologise.	☐	☐
d. This school has certainly put itself on the map.	☐	☐
e. Did you make the dessert yourself?	☐	☐
f. They shouldn't put themselves in danger like that.	☐	☐
g. Jiah needs to look after herself better.	☐	☐
h. I'd like to speak to the managing director himself.	☐	☐
i. We were pleased because we had completed the project ourselves.	☐	☐

 ISBN 978-93-5103-603-6

6. Fill in each blank with a suitable **interrogative pronoun**.

a. ________ invented the Internet?

b. ________ are you doing today?

c. ________ is this mobile phone?

d. ________ of these colours do you prefer?

e. To ________ am I speaking, please?

7. Circle the correct **interrogative pronoun** to complete each sentence.

a. (Who / Whom) rang the doorbell?

b. For (whom / who) was the letter?

c. I want to know (who / whom) told you that?

d. (Who / Whom) offered to help?

e. Ginny had received a gift, and I wanted to know from (who / whom).

f. (Whom / Who) came to school to pick you up yesterday?

g. (Who / Whom) is going to clean up the mess?

h. To (who / whom) shall I address the letter?

i. (Who / Whom) won the match?

j. For (who / whom) are you buying that book?

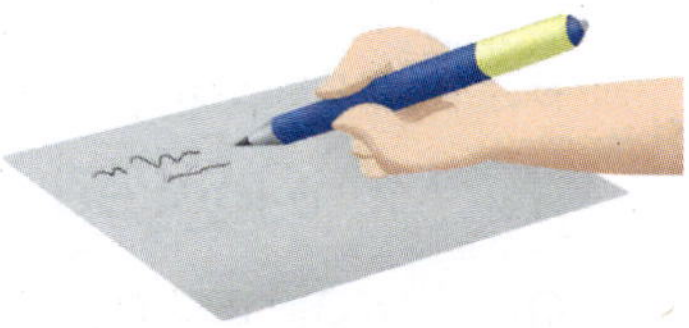

8. Fill in the blanks in the story with suitable **interrogative pronouns**.

The telephone rang as I was dropping off to sleep. ________ could be ringing so late?

"Hello," I said, "________ is that?"

"It's me," said the voice.

"But ________ is me?" I asked.

"Harry," came the reply.

"Harry," I said, "do you know ________ the time is? ________ are you ringing me for at this hour of the night?"

"I had to talk to you," said Harry. "I solved the crossword in 20 minutes flat!"

"Of all the crosswords in all the newspapers, ________ have you solved?"

"The one in *The New York Times*!" said Harry.

"So ________?" was all I could answer.

 ISBN 978-93-5103-603-6

9. Rewrite each sentence adding **the** where necessary.

a. Gaurav chose bigger of the two cakes for his birthday.

____

b. Meeting has been postponed till fifth of July.

____

c. First time I saw Javed he was wrapped up in a blanket.

____

d. What is earliest memory you have?

____

e. This is most expensive watch I have ever seen.

____

f. Which is shorter month, November or December?

____

10. Fill in the blanks in the story with **a**, **an** or **the**.

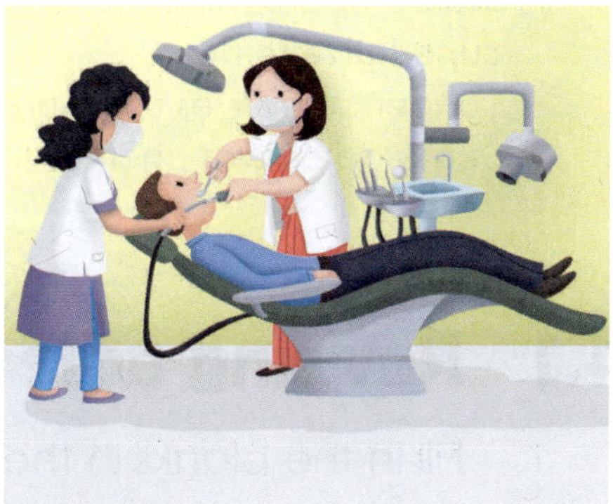

________ last time I had toothache I thought I'd better make ________ appointment at ________ dentist's.

"Is ________ pain very bad?" the receptionist asked.

"Yes," I said, "________ worst I've ever had."

"I'm afraid that ________ earliest appointment I can give you is on ________ seventh of May, in two days' time."

"Is that really ________ first available appointment?" I asked.

"Let me look again," she said. "Ah, there is actually ________ cancellation at 5.30 this evening, ________ last appointment of ________ day."

When ________ dentist examined ________ tooth he said ________ only thing he could do was extract it.

Spot the Error

11. There is a mistake in each sentence. Underline it and rewrite the passage correctly in your notebook.

"Who's is all that rubbish in our trash can on the stairs?" asked Shanti. "Guess we'll have to clear it yourselves," sighed Mum. Shanti and her family lived on an third floor of a block of flats. It was most well maintained of all the buildings in the neighbourhood. Shanti's brother Harsh said, "I think I know whom has dumped their trash there. I'll go and talk to them myselves."

 ISBN 978-93-5103-603-6

4 Adjectives

Let's Recall

- **Adjectives** describe nouns. Some adjectives describe the material, appearance, age, speed, temperature or quality of nouns.
- Adjectives that tell us the amount or quantity of something are called **adjectives of quantity**. They include **adjectives of number**, which tell us the exact amount.
- We use **my**, **our**, **your**, **his**, **her**, **its** and **their** to show or ask who or what possesses or has something. They are called **possessive adjectives**.
- We use **this**, **that**, **these** and **those** to point out particular people or things. They are called **demonstrative adjectives**.
- Adjectives have three forms. When we want to describe someone or something without comparing them with anyone or anything, we use the **positive form**. When we compare two nouns, we add **-r** or **-er** to the adjective. This is known as the **comparative form**. When we compare more than two nouns, we add **-est** to the adjective. This is known as the **superlative form**.
- Longer adjectives use **more** or **most** to form the comparative and superlative.
- Some adjectives change their form completely in the comparative and superlative.

4.1 Revising adjectives

1. Fill in the blanks in the story with suitable **adjectives** from the box below.

exciting	delicious	big	pineapple	old	white	fresh
black	chilled	different	wooden	new		

Jasleen celebrated her tenth birthday last week. She threw a ________ party for her friends. It was a costume party, so all the children dressed up in ________ ways. Jasleen was dressed as an ________ pirate with a wig of ________ hair and a ________ patch over one eye. There were lots of ________ games for the children to play. Jasleen's parents brought out a ________ cake on a ________ tray as everyone sang "Happy Birthday". There was ________ juice and ________ salad and plenty of other ________ food. Jasleen got a ________ bicycle as a birthday gift!

  ISBN 978-93-5103-603-6

2. Fill in each blank with an **adjective of quantity** from the top box and another suitable **adjective** from the lower box.

all	any	a few	a little	many	much	several	some

small	useful	juicy	difficult	rainy	bad	Japanese	chocolate

a. ________ suggestions were made at the meeting.

b. I still have ________ tasks to do.

c. There haven't been ________ days this monsoon season.

d. We didn't have ________ weather during our holiday.

e. I had ________ currency left after my trip.

f. I bought ________ apples at the market.

g. No one asked ________ questions.

h. ________ the ________ biscuits have been eaten.

Take Note

Some adjectives tell us which place or country a person, animal or thing comes from or belongs to, e.g. **Chinese** dumplings, **African** elephant.

3. Fill in each blank with a **possessive adjective**.

a. Komal, keep ________ back straight.

b. Jason has lost ________ exercise book.

c. The Roshans are having ________ house painted.

d. Bhushan and I have bought ________ tickets already.

e. Has Mrs Sharma gone home? ________ shawl isn't here.

f. The cat was chasing ________ tail.

g. I haven't told anyone ________ news yet.

h. Rita and Khushi! Please keep ________ voices down.

4. Circle the **possessive adjective** and fill in the blank with a **possessive pronoun** in each sentence.

a. I've eaten my breakfast. Have you eaten ________ yet?

b. Has everyone got their swimsuit? Paul has lost ________.

c. Jyoti left her doll in the park. I put ________ in my toy box.

d. Your supper is in the oven, Akash. We've had ________.

e. Vishal and I have tidied our desks, but Kajal has left ________ in a mess.

f. Every town has its own character, just as we have ________.

g. Now that Prateek has read us his story, everyone else must read us ________.

h. Where did the Alvas park their car? We parked ________ in Park Street.

Remember!

- The possessive adjectives are **my**, **your**, **his**, **her**, **its**, **our** and **their**.
- The possessive pronouns are **mine**, **yours**, **his**, **hers**, **ours** and **theirs**. They are NOT used before a noun.

 ISBN 978-93-5103-603-6

5. Complete each sentence with a suitable **adjective** from the box below. You may use some adjectives more than once.

some	any	all

a. I'm inviting ________ friends to my party.
b. Sorry, I don't have ________ stamps.
c. The robbers made off with ________ the money in the bank.
d. We managed to get ________ work done in the evening.
e. Is there ________ curry left in the bowl?

Take Note
- Some adjectives can be used for both countable and uncountable nouns, e.g. **some** girls, **some** milk.
- **All** is used with **the** to mean everyone or everything in a group, or the total amount, e.g. **all** the books, **all** the rice.

6. Circle the correct **demonstrative adjective** to complete each sentence.

a. I'd like you to answer (that / this) question honestly.
b. What are (these / those) funny insects over there?
c. Look at (that / this) spot on my arm.
d. Can you see (this / that) tall grey tower?
e. Please listen to (those / these) instructions carefully.
f. I'd like (this / that) car in the shop window.

7. Fill in each blank with a **demonstrative adjective** of your choice and a suitable **adjective** from the box below.

shabby	colourful	silver	plastic	sleepy	unkind

Example I like that colourful picture hanging on the wall.

a. I always wear ________ trousers for gardening.
b. Could you fetch me ________ bucket?
c. Nothing ever happens in ________ town.
d. Did you ever find ________ necklace you lost?
e. You shouldn't have made ________ remarks.

8. Rewrite each sentence adding **all** and a suitable **demonstrative adjective** before the underlined noun.

a. I must dust books on the top shelf.

____

b. I've been asked to give you leaflets.

____

Take Note
The adjective **all** can be used with a demonstrative adjective before a noun, e.g. **all those** words, **all this** work.

 ISBN 978-93-5103-603-6

c. We are being delayed by problems.

____

d. Tell me what fuss is about.

____

e. What a noise sheep are making!

____

9. Fill in each blank with the **comparative** form of the **adjective(s)** given in the brackets.

a. Can't they think of a ______________ name for the baby? (suitable)

b. If you can think of an ______________ method, tell me. (easy)

c. David was the ______________ twin, but Greg was the ______________ one. (clever, handsome)

d. The situation is ______________ than I thought it was. (bad)

e. I've got a ______________ idea than that. (good)

10. Fill in each blank with the **superlative** form of the **adjective(s)** given in the brackets.

a. Today was the ______________ day of my life. (happy)

b. Our cricket team's performance last Saturday was the ______________ of the whole season. (bad)

c. Which is the ______________ bus to catch? (convenient)

d. Do those who eat the ______________ foods have the ______________ lives? (healthy, long)

e. The Gateway of India is Mumbai's ______________ monument. (famous)

11. Fill in each blank with the **superlative** form of the **adjective** given in the brackets. Add a **possessive adjective** before it.

Example I shall be wearing ____________ outfit. (smart)

I shall be wearing my smartest outfit.

a. Our great-grandmother is ____________ relation. (old)

b. Hema, what is the name of ____________ sister? (young)

c. The sun is at ____________ when it is overhead. (strong)

d. Jiah says Maria is ____________ friend. (close)

e. Gautam knows ____________ fault is laziness. (bad)

Take Note

Instead of using **the** with a superlative adjective, we can use a possessive adjective, e.g. **my best** composition.

 ISBN 978-93-5103-603-6

4.2 More about adjectives of quantity

Remember!
We use **a little** and **a few** to describe the amount or quantity of something without giving the exact measurement.

Read the story.

The earthquake destroyed almost **half** the town. **Little** help could be given till the medical teams arrived.

Few buildings were left standing. There were not **enough** people to rescue those trapped below the heavy beams.

Luckily, there was **enough** food and water for the survivors.

Have you ever felt an earthquake? What did you do?

What was the effect of the earthquake?

How many buildings were left standing after the earthquake?

How much food and water was available?

1. Fill in each blank with a suitable adjective from the story above.
   a. After the earthquake, there were ________ buildings that did not collapse.
   b. At first the injured got ________ help but soon medical teams arrived with ________ medical and food supplies.
   c. ________ the boxes contained bottles of water and the rest contained food.

Take Note
Half is a fraction. We can say **half a** kilo, **half the** pupils, **half my** homework or **half these** books. Other fractions are usually used with **of**, e.g. **a quarter of** a loaf, **two-thirds of** the pupils.

2. Circle the correct adjective to complete each sentence.
   a. There weren't (enough / few) eggs to bake a cake.
   b. (Half / Few) the eggs were broken.
   c. You will make (little / enough) progress unless you try harder.
   d. Hari's family was poor and he had (little / few) toys.
   e. Add (few / enough) milk to the mixture to keep it moist.

Enough, **few**, **little** and **half** are adjectives that describe the amount or quantity of something. They are called **adjectives of quantity**.

 ISBN 978-93-5103-603-6

Let's Practise

A. Fill in the blanks in the story with suitable **adjectives of quantity** from the box below. You may use some adjectives more than once.

many	any	enough	a few	much	some	a little	half

Sally is making a cake for the family. She is checking the ingredients she needs. "Let me see, how ________ flour do I need? Ah, yes, ________ a kilo of flour. And how ________ eggs? Oh, yes, I need four eggs. And how ________ sugar? 300 grams of sugar and the same amount of butter. Do I need ________ nuts? Yes, 100 grams of almonds. But I also need ________ dried fruit. Yes, ________ a kilo of dried fruit. That is, 250 grams of raisins and 250 grams of sultanas. I wonder if that is ________ dried fruit? The recipe says add just ________ milk and ________ drops of vanilla essence."

Take Note

- **A few** means "a small number", but **few** means "not many". **Few** is used with plural nouns, e.g. We had **few** reasons to be glad.
- **A little** means "a small amount", but **little** means "not much". **Little** is used with uncountable nouns, e.g. We had **little** water and no food.

B. Fill in each blank with a suitable **adjective** from the box below. You may use some adjectives more than once.

enough	few	a few	half	third	little	a little	four

1. Anna wasn't good at sport and showed ________ interest in it.
2. Have you ________ good players to make up a team?
3. Can you spare me ________ apples? I'd like to make a pie.
4. Azad still had ________ a kilometre left to finish the race.
5. The old man lived alone and had ________ friends.
6. The ________ candidate seems the most suitable for the job.
7. Would you like ________ honey on your toast?
8. There were as many as ________ senior professors on the selection committee.
9. The children have finished off most of the food, but there is ________ stew left for you.

Take Note

- **Adjectives of number** include numbers, fractions and words such as **all** and **many**.
- Numbers such as one, ten and hundred are called **cardinals**.
- Numbers such as first, tenth and hundredth, that show the order of nouns, are called **ordinals**.

 ISBN 978-93-5103-603-6

4.3 Interrogative adjectives

Read the story.

"Mum, **whose** lunch boxes are these?" asked Mike.

Nina opened her lunch box and said, "This isn't my lunch! **What** food do you have in yours, Mike?"

"All these lunch boxes look the same!" said Mike. "Mum, can you please tell us **which** lunch box belongs to **which** person?"

Do you think Mum will be able to sort out the muddle? Why do you think so?

What did Mike ask Mum?

What did Nina ask Mike?

What did Mike ask Mum to do?

Remember!
Sentences that ask a question are called interrogative sentences. Many interrogative sentences begin with **wh- words**, including **what**, **which** and **whose**.

1. Note the highlighted words in the story above. Now use them to complete each question.

   a. __________ lunch box is mine?

   b. __________ lunch boxes are ours?

   c. __________ lunch box is this?

   d. __________ food was in Nina's lunch box?

   e. __________ schoolbags are those?

2. Underline the question word and circle the noun that it asks about.

   a. Which players have been selected for the team?

   b. This isn't my school bag. Whose school bag is it?

   c. Which way do we go, left or right?

   d. Whose belongings are these?

Take Note
- **What** asks for something or someone to be identified from the whole class of people or things, e.g. **What** book are you reading?
- **Which** asks for someone or something to be identified from a known group, e.g. **Which** bicycle is yours?
- **Whose** asks for the owner of something to be identified, e.g. **Whose** purse is this?

What, **which** and **whose** are question words that can be used with nouns to ask for someone or something to be identified. They are called **interrogative adjectives**.

 ISBN 978-93-5103-603-6

Let's Practise

A. Fill in the blanks in the story with suitable **interrogative adjectives**.

Arjun and Anisha walked into the Peacock Restaurant and spoke to the head waiter.

"We booked a table for eight o'clock," said Arjun.

"_______ name did you book the table under?" asked the head waiter.

"Patel," said Arjun. "_______ table is ours? I asked for the one by the window."

"Oh, I'm afraid that table is taken," said the head waiter.

"That's strange," said Arjun, feeling a bit annoyed. "_______ reservation was it? _______ time did they book for?"

"Let me check," said the head waiter. "Oh, they also booked for eight o'clock and their name is Patel too!"

The two couples discussed the situation and laughed.

The head waiter asked, "So _______ couple would like _______ table?"

The two couples exchanged tables, and everyone was happy.

B. Look at the underlined word in each sentence. In the brackets, write **A** if it is an interrogative adjective or **P** if it is an interrogative pronoun.

1. Whose pencil case is this? [ ]
2. Who are you texting? [ ]
3. Which is your car? [ ]
4. What day is it today? [ ]
5. Whose is that bicycle? [ ]
6. What subjects are you studying? [ ]
7. Which road should we take? [ ]
8. What is the time? [ ]

Take Note

Interrogative adjectives are used before a noun. Interrogative pronouns are used in place of nouns.

C. Make sentences with the **interrogative adjectives** given below, using nouns from the box.

path	boots	number

1. What ____
2. Whose ____
3. Which ____

 ISBN 978-93-5103-603-6

4.4 Emphasising adjectives

Read the story.

Mr Harris looked at the skyscrapers in **utter** amazement. He found the **whole** place a **complete** mystery.

When he went to get a good view of the city from a rooftop, he saw an **absolute** muddle of buildings.

In his **own** opinion, the best view is from a bridge or hilltop at the **very** edge of the city.

Do you think Mr Harris belonged to the city?

What did Mr Harris feel when he looked at the skyscrapers?

What did he see from the rooftop?

Where does Mr Harris think is the best place to get a good view of a city?

1. Note the highlighted words in the story above. Now circle the word that emphasises or gives special importance to the underlined noun in each sentence.

   a. A good view of the city is an absolute delight.

   b. The whole place was a mystery to him.

   c. If you want your visit to a new city to be a complete success, look for a hilltop to view it from a distance.

2. Fill in each blank with a suitable word pair from the box below.

absolute beauty	total waste	whole time	utter nuisance

   a. People who are always late are an ____________________.

   b. Pete's new sports car is an ____________________!

   c. Trying to get rid of weeds is a ____________________ of energy.

   d. Dinesh and Sonal spent the ____________________ arguing.

Words such as **whole, complete, total, absolute, own, utter** and **very** are often used with nouns to strengthen or emphasise them. They are called **emphasising adjectives**.

 ISBN 978-93-5103-603-6

Let's Practise

A. Circle the correct **emphasising adjective** to complete each sentence.

1. The doctor said that I should have a (complete / utter) break for a month.
2. I don't want to spend the (total / whole) day sightseeing.
3. He had lost his money and was facing (utter / whole) ruin.
4. I shouldn't have bought that dress. It was a (complete / whole) mistake.
5. His house is the furthest away in the colony. It is at the (complete / very) end of the road.
6. The concert was an (utter / absolute) triumph.

Take Note

- The adjective **whole** is often used to emphasise the length of a period of time, e.g. He spent the **whole** day in bed.
- The adjective **own** is used to emphasise possession, e.g. This is my **own** bedroom.

B. Fill in the blanks in the story with suitable **emphasising adjectives** from the box below.

whole	complete	utter	absolute	entire

I'm glad to say that my trip to Venice was a ____________ success. The guide who showed us round was an ____________ marvel. She seemed to have an ____________ encyclopaedia of local information in her head. That meant we didn't have to spend the ____________ time trying to find things out for ourselves. The food was wonderful too. The trip was an ____________ delight for all of us.

C. Rewrite each sentence using an **emphasising adjective** of your choice in the correct position.

1. The newspaper critic treated the play as a joke.

   ____

2. That's nonsense!

   ____

3. The traffic came to a standstill.

   ____

4. I'm telling you the truth.

   ____

5. We all have our problems to deal with.

   ____

 ISBN 978-93-5103-603-6

4.5 Adjective phrases

Remember!
A phrase is a group of words that has meaning but does not make complete sense.

Read the story.

Simon looked out of his window and saw a **quite unfamiliar** car outside.

He felt **rather frightened** when a man **with dark glasses** walked up the front path.

Wearing a helmet and **armed with a baseball bat**, Simon opened the door. The man merely handed Simon his business card.

How do you think Simon felt when the man gave him the card?

What did Simon see outside his window?

How did he feel when he saw the man?

What words are used to describe Simon when he opened the door?

1. Note the highlighted phrases in the story above. Now underline the phrase that describes a noun in each sentence.
   a. There was a completely unfamiliar car out in the road.
   b. A man in dark glasses came up the path.
   c. Armed with a baseball bat, Simon waited for the man to ring the doorbell.

2. Fill in the blanks with suitable phrases from the box below.

in the white suit	rather old	smiling happily	in that flat	very fierce

Example ____________________, Priya ran to meet Dad.

Smiling happily, Priya ran to meet Dad.

a. The family ____________________ have a ____________________ dog.

b. The man ____________________ shook hands with me.

c. Mum drives a ____________________ car.

A group of words that functions as an adjective and describes a noun or pronoun in a sentence is called an **adjective phrase**.

 ISBN 978-93-5103-603-6

Let's Practise

A. Fill in each blank with a suitable **adjective phrase** from the box below.

terribly boring	smartly dressed	neatly written
badly trained	pretty clever	

1. Sarika is a ____________ student. She always gets good grades.
2. A ____________ lady got off the train at Nagpur.
3. Be careful! That dog is ____________ and might harm you.
4. It's always a pleasure to read a ____________ composition.
5. It's a ____________ film. Don't go and see it.

B. Rewrite each sentence, changing the underlined words into an **adjective phrase**.

Example The lady <u>who has blonde hair</u> sat next to me.
<u>The lady with blonde hair sat next to me.</u>

1. The man <u>who has a walking stick</u> is the owner of this mansion.
____
2. The woman <u>who has a red coat</u> is my English teacher.
____
3. The passengers <u>who are on the bus</u> are all from Jaipur.
____
4. The girl <u>who is at the reception desk</u> is my friend's cousin.
____

Take Note
Adjective phrases can
- come before a noun and often include adverbs, e.g. a **warmly clothed** child.
- come after a noun, e.g. the lady **in the seat next to me**.
- come after a verb such as **be** or **become**, e.g. Are you **ready for a surprise**? She became **interested in science**.

Remember!
A phrase is a group of words that does not have a subject or a predicate.

C. Underline the **adjective phrases** in the sentences below.

1. The boy sitting on my right is a school prefect.
2. I love ice cream made with real cream.
3. The people listening to the concert all enjoy classical music.
4. The books piled in that corner have to be packed.
5. The mobile phone lying on the table is Dad's.

Take Note
Adjective phrases can
- begin with a present participle, e.g. I looked at the baby **sleeping peacefully in his cot**.
- begin with a past participle, e.g. Hannah arrived **dressed all in red**.

Think & Share Pair up with a classmate to play "The Sentence Game". Start with a simple sentence, for example, The man crossed the road. Then each of you take turns to expand the sentence by adding adjective phrases. For example, The man in the blue coat with curly hair sipping a juice crossed the road.

 ISBN 978-93-5103-603-6

5 Verbs

Let's Recall

- Doing and being words are called **verbs**. A **tense** is a form taken by a verb to show the time of an action. There are three main tenses, the **present**, the **past** and the **future**.
- We use the **simple present tense** to talk about facts, habits and actions that happen in the present. We use the **simple past tense** to report actions in the past. We use the **simple future tense** to talk about things that are going to happen.
- We use the **present continuous tense** for an activity going on at present. We use the **past continuous tense** to report an action that continued for some time in the past. We use the **future continuous tense** to talk about activities that will be happening at a certain point in the future.
- We use the **present perfect tense** to talk about an action that happened in the past, but still affects the present. We use the **past perfect tense** to report something that happened before the time we are talking about. We use the **future perfect tense** to talk about activities that will be over by a particular time in the future.
- The **present participle** is the **-ing** form of a verb. It can be used in the continuous tenses, and also as an adjective. The **past participle** is the **-ed** form of a verb. It can be used in the perfect tenses, and also as an adjective.
- We use **could** to talk about ability and for making suggestions, **should** to give advice and to talk about expected happenings, **might** for warnings and guesses, and **must** to say that there is something that we simply have to do and for saying what is likely.

5.1 Revising verbs

1. Fill in each blank with the **simple present** form of the **verb** given in the brackets.
   a. Mr Gupta ________ us Science. (teach)
   b. The bridge ________ the railway over the river. (carry)
   c. Dina ________ very gracefully. (dance)
   d. The bus ________ our house. (pass)
   e. Sheela ________ several miles on foot to get to school. (journey)

2. Fill in each blank with the **simple past** form of the **verb** given in the brackets.
   a. Mrs Verma ________ a new laptop yesterday. (buy)
   b. I ________ my hair last night. (shampoo)
   c. Rina ________ to give me your message. (forget)
   d. Hari's horse ________ home to win. (gallop)

 ISBN 978-93-5103-603-6

3. Circle the correct form of the **verb** to complete each sentence.

   a. The hotel price usually (included / includes) breakfast.

   b. The Lilliputians (fasten / fastened) Gulliver to the ground with ropes.

   c. The baby often (echoes / echoed) people's words.

   d. Oliver Twist (dares / dared) to ask for a second helping of food.

   e. We (went / go) to the supermarket once a week.

4. Fill in the blanks with the **present continuous** form of the **verb** given in the brackets.

   > **Take Note**
   > The present continuous tense can be used for planned future actions.

   a. Tomorrow we __________ the children to the museum. (take)

   b. What __________ your brother __________ at university? (study)

   c. I __________ a surprise for Leila's birthday. (plan)

   d. Why __________ those two __________? (argue)

   e. Who __________ you __________ to? (refer)

   f. We __________ the book for publication. (edit)

5. Fill in the blanks with the **past continuous** form of the **verb** given in the brackets.

   a. I __________ my bike along the road when my tyre burst. (pedal)

   b. The hairdresser talked to me while she __________ my hair. (cut)

   c. We __________ round the park when it began to rain. (jog)

   d. What __________ you __________ to Deepak about just then? (whisper)

   e. Why __________ Jamila __________? Had she hurt herself? (cry)

   f. __________ you __________ to contact me yesterday? (try)

6. Fill in the blanks in the story with the **present continuous** or the **past continuous** form of the **verbs** given in the brackets.

Kirti __________ (lie) on the sofa when Dev walked into the living room. She __________ (watch) a programme on the television, and __________ (hold) the remote in her hand. "What __________ you __________ (do) indoors on such a lovely afternoon?" asked Dev. "I __________ just __________ (rest)," said Kirti. "Well," said Dev, "I __________ (set) off for a healthy walk now. __________ you __________ (come) with me or __________ you __________ (stay) here?" Kirti agreed that she __________ (waste) the lovely weather and joined Dev for his walk.

 ISBN 978-93-5103-603-6

7. Fill in the blanks with the **present perfect** form of the **verb** given in the brackets.

a. When you ________ that exercise, you may sit and read quietly. (finish)

b. ________ you ________ the children properly for the expedition? (equip)

c. I ________ my wallet, so I can't pay for lunch. (lose)

d. What ________ you ________ to your hair? It looks really awful. (do)

e. Why ________ Hemant ________ himself in his room again? (lock)

f. I must go shopping because we ________ out of food. (run)

8. Fill in the blanks with the **past perfect** form of the **verb** given in the brackets.

a. I looked at the clock and realised that I ________ for twelve hours. (sleep)

b. We knew we ________ the perfect place for a holiday. (find)

c. It ________ in the night, so the air felt fresh. (rain)

d. I ________ not ________ the book they were discussing. (read)

e. Jamil thought he ________ his leg, but it was fine. (break)

f. Divya gave us each a piece of the cake she ________. (bake)

9. Fill in the blanks in the story with the **present perfect** or the **past perfect** form of the **verbs** given in the brackets.

Sania and Vijay were busy packing their suitcases for a trip to Malaysia. They ________ already ________ (lay) everything out ready the night before, but were still anxious in case they ________ (forget) anything. "________ you ________ (pack) your swimming things?" asked Sania. "Of course," said Vijay, "but what ________ you ________ (do) with the passports? I can't see them anywhere." "I ________ already ________ (put) them in my handbag," said Sania. "And what about the air tickets?" asked Vijay. "I hope you ________ not ________ (hide) them at the bottom of a suitcase." "I ________ (slip) those safely in my handbag too," said Sania. When they were absolutely certain they ________ (stow) everything they needed into the right bags and suitcases, they looked at each other. "I think it's time to call the taxi," said Sania.

 ISBN 978-93-5103-603-6

10. Fill in the blanks in each sentence with the **simple future** form of the **verb** given in the brackets.

a. _______ we _______ travel insurance for our holiday? (need)

b. What _______ you _______ in the report? (write)

c. _______ they _______ time to visit us? (have)

d. What _______ your mum _______ when she sees you? (say)

Remember!
We use **shall** with first person pronouns and **will** with all other personal pronouns.

11. Rewrite each sentence using the short form **'ll**.

a. I shall meet you tomorrow at the school gates.

____

b. You will enjoy your visit to Mauritius.

____

c. We shall bring the kebabs for the barbecue.

____

d. It will be a pleasure to meet Poonam again.

____

12. Fill in the blanks with the **future continuous** form of the **verb** given in the brackets. Use the short form **'ll** where you can.

a. We ____________ house in two weeks' time. (move)

b. _______ you ____________ Dina tomorrow? (see)

c. I ____________ a chemist if you want any medicine. (pass)

d. _______ we ____________ by bus or train? (travel)

e. _______ it ____________ in Scotland just now? (snow)

Take Note
The simple future and future continuous tenses are used to state plans and decisions. Another way of expressing plans for the future is to use **be going to**, e.g. We **are going to start** swimming lessons next week.

13. Fill in the blanks with the **future perfect** form of the **verb** given in the brackets. Use the short form **'ll** where you can.

a. By 5.00 p.m. tomorrow we ____________ in Sydney. (land)

b. _______ the schools ____________ to winter timings by 1 November? (change)

c. I ____________ school by 2020. (leave)

d. Surely Bill and Sue ____________ our message by now? (receive)

e. It'll be good to see the children – how they ____________ since we last saw them! (grow)

14. Circle the correct **verb** to complete each sentence below.

a. The weather (might / must) improve.

b. You (should / might) keep a list of incoming calls.

 ISBN 978-93-5103-603-6

c. The bell has rung. You (must / might) stop writing now.

d. I (could / should) swim by the time I was five.

15. Rewrite each sentence, changing the underlined verbs into the **continuous tense**.

Example People will gossip about this.

People will be gossiping about this.

a. Mum always tidied the house.

____

b. Sara wears glasses.

____

c. The wind blew through the streets.

____

d. Will you cancel the match?

____

16. Fill in the blanks in the story with the **present participles** of suitable **verbs** from the box below.

sing	run	shine	cook	play	pull	stand
fall	rescue	pant	lose	look	swim	

Mum was in the kitchen _______ lunch while the baby was _______ in a corner. The sun was _______ in through the window, and there was the sound of birds _______ in the trees. Suddenly Sara came _______ in, _______ and _______ very excited. "Your hair and clothes are wet! Have you been _______ somewhere?" asked Mum. "No, Mum, I've been _______ a little kid from the pond. I saw him _______ in, and I was _______ on the bank _______ him out when I found I was _______ my balance myself. So I fell in too. Then his mum appeared and helped us get out."

17. Look at the underlined word in each sentence. In the brackets, write **V** if it is a verb or **A** if it is an adjective.

a. Mum, you are always worrying about something. [ ]

b. We now have some breaking news from Thailand. [ ]

c. These are exciting times. [ ]

d. No more nasty stories. You are terrifying the children. [ ]

 ISBN 978-93-5103-603-6

18. Rewrite each sentence, changing the **simple past** into the **present perfect**.

a. I swam three lengths of the pool.

____

b. Did you finish that exercise?

____

c. What did you do with the photos?

____

d. Did Dad lose his wallet?

____

e. Gina went home.

____

19. Fill in the blanks in the story with the **past participles** of suitable **verbs** from the box below.

Remember!
Present and past participles can be used as adjectives.

be	close	leave	drive	forget	drop	visit
puzzle	begin	walk	park	see		

It was a mystery. Dad had ______ us outside the museum, and then had ______ off to park the car. Mum took us all into the museum. We had already ______ several different rooms when Dad arrived. He had ______ the car in a nearby street and ______ all the way back to the museum. When we had ______ a few more of the exhibits, the bell rang to say that the museum was now ______. Out we went. Dad looked ______. Where had he ______ the car? He had ______ the street name, but not completely. It had ______ with M. We looked at the map and realised it must have ______ Menon Street! And that was where we found the car!

20. Fill in each blank with the **present** or **past participle** form of the **verb** given in the brackets.

a. This has been a very ______ day. (bore)

b. Yasmin had a ______ expression on her face. (worry)

c. I'm afraid I have ______ news for you. (disturb)

d. Are you ______ in dinosaurs? (interest)

e. Yes, I find dinosaurs ______. (fascinate)

 ISBN 978-93-5103-603-6

5.2 Transitive verbs

Remember!
In a sentence, the subject is the noun, pronoun or group of words that the sentence is about. The predicate is the part of the sentence that contains the verb.

Read the story.

Mr Brown **owned** a fine orchard in which he **grew** apple trees.

In the autumn he **employed** helpers to **pick** the apples.

Then he **put** the apples into barrels, and **sold** them from a roadside stall.

What do you think is Mr Brown's profession?

What did Mr Brown do in his orchard?

What did the helpers do in the autumn?

What did Mr Brown do with the apples?

1. Read the story again. Now match each underlined verb in the first column with the correct answer in the second column.

a. What did Mr Brown own?	•	•	i. helpers
b. What did Mr Brown grow?	•	•	ii. an orchard
c. Whom did Mr Brown employ?	•	•	iii. apples

2. Circle the verb showing an action, underline the person doing the action, and double-underline the thing or person that receives the action in each sentence.

   Example Diana opened the window.

   a. Ramesh swept the floor.
   b. Mum hugged Kamal.
   c. Dad read the letter.
   d. The doctor examined my leg.
   e. I cooked the pasta.
   f. An old man rang the doorbell.

Take Note
The person or thing that does the action is the **subject** of the verb, e.g. **You** hurt me. The thing or person that receives the action or that the action affects is the **object** of the verb, e.g. You hurt **me**.

A verb that has an object is called a **transitive verb**.

 ISBN 978-93-5103-603-6

Let's Practise

A. Answer each question by choosing an **object** from the box to go with the underlined **transitive verb**.

water	the eggs	us	the table	Suresh's mum	their names

Example What did Deepak hit with his fist?

Deepak hit the table with his fist.

1. What did Nita carry home carefully?

   ____

2. What should you drink after every meal?

   ____

3. Whom did you meet in the supermarket?

   ____

4. Whom did Dad take to the museum?

   ____

5. What should they write at the top of the page?

   ____

Take Note
To test if a verb has an object we can ask "What?" or "Whom?" after saying the verb. If there is an answer in the sentence, the verb is transitive.

B. Circle the **transitive verb** and underline its **object** in each sentence.

1. Ring the bell three times.
2. We watched a programme about global warming.
3. Jenny helped me with my homework.
4. We found a short route back to the hotel.
5. The magic spell turned the wicked witch into a snake.
6. I'll wear the dress with the flowery pattern.
7. We'll use the yellow mugs today.
8. Please put the spoons away in the drawer.

Take Note
The object of a verb may be a noun, a pronoun or a group of words, e.g. Please fetch (verb) **that book with the red cover** (object).

C. Fill in each blank with the simple past form of a suitable **transitive verb** from the box below. Then circle its **object**.

paint	book	drink	read	delete

1. Rina __________ three glasses of juice.
2. I __________ all the messages.
3. We __________ Chapter Five in class today.
4. Najma __________ a picture of a rough sea.
5. They __________ two seats for the concert.

Remember!
A sentence is divided into a subject and a predicate. The object of the verb is part of the predicate, e.g. **You** (subject) **hurt me** (predicate).

 ISBN 978-93-5103-603-6

5.3 Verbs and their objects

Read the story.

Mr Pinto is fixing Mrs Pinto some breakfast on her birthday. He pours her a cup of tea.

Next he makes her some hot buttered toast.

The tray shakes dangerously as he bounds upstairs to give his wife her breakfast.

Do you think Mrs Pinto will be pleased when she gets her breakfast?

What is Mr Pinto making? For whom is he making it?

What does he do after pouring the tea?

Why does he go upstairs?

1. Note the highlighted sets of words in the story above. Now circle the object of the verb in each sentence and underline the noun or pronoun that shows who the object is meant for.

Example Mr Pinto brought his wife breakfast.

a. Mr Pinto poured his wife a cup of tea.

b. He bought her a red rose.

c. He made her some toast.

d. He gave her the breakfast tray.

2. Look at the underlined object in each sentence. Then rewrite the sentence, adding the object given in the brackets to say who it is meant for.

Example Children! Give flowers now and then. (your mothers)

Children! Give your mothers flowers now and then.

a. Please read a story. (me)

____

b. Let me tell my news. (you)

____

c. A polite boy offered his seat. (the elderly lady)

____

d. The waitress brought our lunch. (us)

____

Transitive verbs can have more than one object. The thing or person that is directly affected by the action is the **direct object**, for example, I told a **story**. The person to whom the object is given, or for whom the action is done, is the **indirect object**, for example, I told **Michael** a story.

 ISBN 978-93-5103-603-6

Let's Practise

A. Circle the **verb** and underline its **direct object** in each sentence.

1. Vishal gave his sister a new dress.
2. Mum has bought Vicky a new hat.
3. Who sent me this card?
4. The doctor gave Amrita some medicine.

Take Note
The direct object usually comes after the indirect object.

B. Circle the **verb** and underline the **indirect object** in each sentence.

1. The professor gave her students tips.
2. Bina asked the teacher a question.
3. The doctor passed her assistant the report.
4. The manager sent his employees Diwali gifts.

Remember!
The person to whom the object is given, or for whom the action is done, is the indirect object.

C. Rewrite each sentence, replacing the underlined **indirect object** with a phrase beginning with **to** or **for**.

Example I handed Mum the plate.
I handed the plate to Mum.

1. Could you make me a cup of coffee?
____
2. The bank sent all its customers a letter.
____
3. Deepak showed Komal the photos.
____

Take Note
We can use the prepositions **to** or **for** with a noun or pronoun to indicate the indirect object. So, instead of saying, "I made **Mum** breakfast," we can say, "I made breakfast **for Mum**."

D. Rewrite each sentence, replacing the underlined words with an **indirect object**.

Example Fetch the dictionary for me.
Fetch me the dictionary.

1. The manager found a job for Peter.
____
2. Miss Lee read a story to her class.
____
3. Nina wrote a letter to her cousin.
____

Think & Share Pair up with a classmate. Make a list of ten nouns and pronouns. Arrange ten items from the classroom on a table. Take turns to make funny sentences using a noun or pronoun (indirect object) from the list and an item from the table (direct object). For example, Harsh gave the cat a ruler.

 ISBN 978-93-5103-603-6

5.4 Intransitive verbs

Read the story.

Dora and Dan **were** both **competing** in the drawing competition.

Dora **laughed** at Dan's drawing. Dan **started** again and drew another lion.

Both Dora and Dan got prizes, but Dan **did** better.

Who do you think got first prize?

Why were Dora and Dan drawing?

What did Dora do when she saw Dan's drawing?

How do you think Dora felt when she received second prize?

1. Note the highlighted verbs in the story above. Now look at the pairs of sentences. Tick the sentence with a transitive verb.
   a. i. Dora and Dan were drawing for the art competition. [ ]
      ii. Dan was drawing a lion. [ ]
   b. i. Dan started again. [ ]
      ii. Dan started a new drawing. [ ]
   c. i. Dan won the trophy. [ ]
      ii. Dan won easily. [ ]

Remember!
A verb that has an object that receives the action of the verb is called a transitive verb. To test if a verb has an object we can ask "What?" or "Whom?" after saying the verb. If there is an answer in the sentence, the verb has an object.

2. Complete each sentence with a verb or a phrase from the box below.

waited	read	arrived	through the woods	across the river	in the gym

   a. Ben has been exercising ________________.
   b. Please ________________ to the end of the chapter.
   c. We walked ________________.
   d. I ________________ for an hour.
   e. Harry swam ________________.
   f. Your letter ________________ this morning.

A verb that has no object is called an **intransitive verb**. Such verbs are often followed by phrases.

 ISBN 978-93-5103-603-6

Let's Practise

A. Underline the **intransitive verbs** in the story below.

Vikram climbed out of bed, stood upright and stretched. He changed out of his pyjamas and into his gym kit. Then he went down to the gym and exercised on various pieces of equipment for an hour. He ran on the treadmill, rowed on the rowing machine and cycled on the training bicycle. Then he jogged back to his apartment, showered and dressed in a smart suit for the office. He breakfasted on cereal and fruit, and then walked to work.

B. Look at the underlined word(s) in each sentence. In the brackets, write **T** if it is a transitive verb or **I** if it is an intransitive verb.

1. Shanti is studying hard for her exams. [ ]
2. Which pilot is flying the aircraft? [ ]
3. Sara is reading quietly in a corner. [ ]
4. I shall be studying Mathematics at university. [ ]
5. Sanjay sang "Happy Birthday" to his mum. [ ]
6. The children played happily in the garden. [ ]
7. Seagulls flew about overhead, wheeling and shrieking. [ ]
8. Rajiv sings in a choir. [ ]
9. Read the poem aloud, please. [ ]
10. We played dominoes till bedtime. [ ]

Take Note

- An intransitive verb is often followed by an adverb phrase.
- Test if a verb is intransitive by saying "What?" or "Whom?" after saying the verb. If there is no answer, then the verb is intransitive.

C. Fill in each blank with a **verb** from the box below. Then underline the **intransitive verbs** and circle the **transitive verbs**. You can use each verb more than once.

change	lost	blew	dressed

1. We ______________ 3-2.
2. We ______________ the match.
3. Sara ______________ quickly in a blue sari.
4. Mum ______________ the baby.
5. I'm going to ______________ for dinner.
6. I'm going to ______________ my library book.
7. The wind ______________ all day.
8. The umpire ______________ his whistle.

 ISBN 978-93-5103-603-6

5.5 Incomplete verbs

Read the story.

Ellie **is** good at the piano and practises hard.

She **will become** a pianist one day, she hopes.

She will perform in public and people **will think** her a great musician.

What does Ellie dream of?

What is Ellie good at?

What does she want to be?

What does she want people to think?

1. Note the highlighted verbs and phrases in the story above. Now underline the verb in the following sentences. Then choose a suitable word or phrase from the box below to complete each sentence.

a great musician	a pianist	talented	good at the piano	ambitious

a. Ellie is ________________.

b. Ellie hopes to become ________________.

c. People will think her ________________.

d. Ellie is ________________.

e. Ellie is ________________.

2. Circle the verb in each sentence and underline the word or phrase that completes its meaning.

Example The sky (grew) very dark.

a. Our teacher is patient with us.

b. The crowd became excited.

c. The increasing traffic is a problem.

d. The teacher appears pleased.

e. Sonal seems tired.

f. Ruchi felt foolish.

Take Note

Verbs such as **be, become** and **seem** link the subject to the description that follows it and completes the sentence.

A verb that needs the help of another word or phrase to complete its meaning in the sentence is called an **incomplete verb**. The word or phrase that forms the predicate and completes what is said about the subject is called the **complement**.

 ISBN 978-93-5103-603-6

Let's Practise

A. Circle the **incomplete verb** in each sentence and underline its **complement**.

Example Rubina seems upset.

1. Your dress looks wonderful.
2. Shashi felt disappointed.
3. That seems a shame.
4. The plant grew tall.
5. The party was a success.
6. Dinner smells delicious.
7. Get well soon.
8. Vijay became a doctor.

B. Double-underline the **complement** that goes with the underlined **object** of the circled **verb** in each sentence.

Example I consider this job a waste of time.

1. Hari set the rabbit free.
2. Who are you calling lazy?
3. What colour shall we paint the walls?
4. I declare the exhibition open.
5. The thunder made me scared.
6. The people elected Hamid mayor.

C. Complete each sentence with a suitable **complement** from the box below.

a punctual person	very close	better
late	transparent	a hero

1. You're making me ____________________.
2. I consider myself ____________________.
3. Are you feeling ____________________?
4. The material looked ____________________.
5. The thunder sounded ____________________.
6. What made him ____________________?

Take Note
To find out if a verb is incomplete, we can omit the description that follows it and check if the sentence still makes complete sense. E.g. The food **looks** appetising. If we omit **appetising** from the sentence, it will not make any sense. So **looks** is an incomplete verb.

Take Note
- If the complement refers to the subject of the verb, it is a **subject complement**. Intransitive verbs can only have subject complements, e.g. Akbar was a **great ruler**.
- If the complement refers to the object of the verb, it is an **object complement**, e.g. The teacher made me **the monitor**.

 ISBN 978-93-5103-603-6

5.6 Participle phrases

Remember!
The **-ing** form of a verb is called the present participle.
The **-ed** form of a verb is called the past participle.

Read the story.

Laura saw the postman **going out of the gate**. Maybe there was a letter **waiting for her**.

She found an envelope **lying on the doormat**.

Opening the envelope, Laura found it was empty! **Puzzled by this**, she stood there, **scratching her head**.

What do you think Laura did next?

What made Laura think she might have a letter?

Where was the envelope?

What did Laura do when she saw the empty envelope?

1. Note the highlighted phrases in the story above. Now underline the phrases that begin with a present or past participle in each sentence.
   - a. Standing at the window, Laura spotted the postman.
   - b. There was an envelope lying on the doormat, addressed to Laura.
   - c. Shaking the envelope vigorously, Laura found nothing in it.

2. Complete the phrase in each sentence with a present or past participle from the box below.

sitting	thrilled	walking	answering	annoyed	picking

   - a. Dad sat at his computer, __________ his e-mails.
   - b. __________ by the delay, he hooted the car horn.
   - c. __________ to be on holiday, the children rushed out of the school.
   - d. __________ on a bench, I watched people __________ to and fro.
   - e. __________ up a pen, Shanti signed her name.

Phrases that begin with a present or past participle are called **participle phrases**. They relate to a noun or pronoun in the sentence.

 ISBN 978-93-5103-603-6

Let's Practise

A. Underline the **participle phrase** in each sentence.

1. The car blocking the road was removed by the police.
2. We could see the white buildings shining in the sunlight.
3. Children encouraged at home by their parents perform much better in school.
4. Opening the door of the laboratory, he got a terrible shock.
5. We'd better join those people waiting in the queue.
6. Written by Lewis Carroll in 1865, *Alice's Adventures in Wonderland* is still popular.
7. He hurried on, looking now and then at his watch.
8. The people waiting for the bus got very wet.

B. Fill in each blank with the correct **present** or **past participle** form of a suitable **verb** from the box below. Then underline the whole **participle phrase**.

reject	paint	sit	wear	try	amaze

1. Speak to the manager. That's the man ________ a grey suit.
2. We specialise in presenting plays ________ by other theatres.
3. The people ________ in the cheaper seats don't get a very good view.
4. I noticed a boy ________ to steal a car.
5. Pictures ________ by M F Husain are very recognisable.
6. Mum sat down suddenly, ________ at the news.

Take Note

Participle phrases can act like adjectives, describing a noun or pronoun. They can refer to a subject or an object, e.g.

- **I** (subject) watched the bird, **impressed by its beauty** (participle phrase referring to **I**).
- I recognised **the lady** (object) **sitting next to me** (participle phrase referring to **the lady**).

C. Underline the **participle phrase** in each sentence.

1. Feeling rather nervous, Rajiv waited to hear his exam results.
2. I always enjoy food cooked over an open fire.
3. Under the tree stood a camel, taking shelter from the heat.
4. The man driving the car looked familiar.
5. Kneeling down, Sita spoke to the child.
6. They fed and educated all the children left in their care.
7. I found the sari hanging over a branch.
8. We visited our grandmother's house, now lying empty and neglected.

 ISBN 978-93-5103-603-6

5.7 Gerunds

Read the story.

Harry and Annie enjoyed **walking** past the pond after **shopping** at the supermarket with Mum.

Finding a frog was something they hadn't expected.

They thought that **scaring** Mum by **showing** her the frog was very funny.

Do you think Mum thought it was funny? What do you think she said to them?

What did Harry and Annie enjoy doing?

Where did Harry and Annie go with Mum?

What did they think was funny?

Remember!
The present participle is an **-ing** form of the verb. It is used in the continuous tenses or as an adjective.

1. Note the highlighted **-ing** words in the story above. Now circle the **-ing** word that plays the role of a noun in each sentence.

   Example They didn't enjoy (shopping) with Mum.

   a. Walking past the pond was great fun.

   b. Finding a frog was even better fun.

   c. Scaring Mum with the frog was the best fun of all.

   d. Poor Mum felt like screaming with fright.

2. Fill in each blank with a suitable word from the box below.

exercising	drinking	swimming	eating

   a. ____________ too much junk food is unhealthy.

   b. You can improve your health by ____________ plenty of water.

   c. ____________ in the gym strengthens your muscles.

   d. His good health is a result of ____________ ten lengths every day.

Besides being the present participle, the **-ing** form of a verb can also function as a noun in a sentence. When it is used in this way, it is called a **verbal noun** or **gerund**.

 ISBN 978-93-5103-603-6

Let's Practise

A. Underline the **gerunds** in the story below.

Rohit was tired of sitting at his desk and doing his homework. Learning Maths and English was very difficult and very dull. He decided that swimming would be more fun, but the pool was closed today. He would have to do something else as a way of banishing the homework blues. Jogging? Playing tennis? Rohit badly needed a break.

> **Take Note**
> To identify an **-ing** form as a gerund, we can ask the question **"What?"** after the verb, e.g. I like (**what?**) cooking.

B. Complete each sentence with a **gerund** using the verb given in the brackets.

Example I intend ____________. (compete)

I intend <u>competing in the Annual Sports Day this year</u>.

1. It began ______________________. (rain)
2. I prefer ______________________. (eat)
3. Dad can't bear ______________________. (waste)
4. I hate ______________________. (disappoint)
5. I like ______________________. (get)
6. I love ______________________. (meet)

> **Take Note**
> A gerund can be
> - the subject of a verb (**Singing** cheers you up.).
> - the object of a verb (I enjoy **singing**.).
> - followed by an object (I like **singing pop songs**.).
> - the object of a preposition (I cheer myself up by **singing**.).

C. Look at the **-ing** word in each sentence. In the brackets, write **G** if it is a gerund or **P** if it is a participle.

1. A swimming dolphin is a delightful sight. [ ]
2. Swimming helps to build muscles. [ ]
3. The jasmine is a climbing plant with a sweet perfume. [ ]
4. Climbing trees used to be my childhood hobby. [ ]
5. Madhu needs a new pair of running shoes. [ ]
6. I could hear running feet in the street outside. [ ]
7. Pritam plans to join a dancing class in the summer. [ ]
8. Dancing couples circled round the floor. [ ]

> **Take Note**
> If the **-ing** form means "doing the activity" (e.g. **sleeping** children), it is a participle.
> If it means "for the activity" (e.g. a **sleeping** bag) it is a gerund.

Think & Share Play the "Gerund Pantomime" game. In a box, place flash cards with gerunds written on them, for example, **reading**, **swimming**, **fishing**. Each student has to pick a gerund and act it out for the class to guess. Whoever guesses correctly has to make a sentence with the gerund.

 ISBN 978-93-5103-603-6

6 Adverbs

Let's Recall

- **Adverbs** tell us more about verbs.
- Adverbs that tell us the manner in which an action is done are called **adverbs of manner**. They are usually formed by adding **-ly** to the adjective.
- Adverbs that tell us the place of an action are called **adverbs of place**.
- Adverbs that tell us the time of an action are called **adverbs of time**.
- Adverbs that tell us how often an action takes or does not take place are called **adverbs of frequency**.
- Adverbs have a **comparative** and a **superlative** form. We form the comparative and superlative of adverbs using **more** and **most**. A few adverbs have a comparative and superlative form ending with **-er** and **-est**. Some adverbs have an **irregular** comparative and superlative.

6.1 Revising adverbs

1. Fill in each blank with an **adverb of manner** formed from an adjective from the box below.

careful	magic	humble	nervous	noisy

a. Anu stood _________ on the starting line.

b. Sara steered the boat _________ round the rocks.

c. He knelt _________ before the king.

d. The children ran about shouting _________.

e. The frog was transformed _________ back into a prince.

2. Fill in the blanks in the story with suitable **adverbs of place**, **time** or **frequency** from the box below.

above	soon	now	then	inside	everywhere	outside

My uncle has a farm in the country. It's so beautiful, with the blue sky _________, and grass _________. I'd like to be a farmer and work _________ in the fresh air. It will _________ be the holidays. _________ I'll go and help my uncle on the farm. But _________ I have to stay _________ and do my homework.

 ISBN 978-93-5103-603-6

3. Rewrite each sentence using the **adverb of frequency** given in the brackets.

a. I make promises! (never)

____

b. The birds wake me up in the morning. (often)

____

c. Vijay takes the train to university. (always)

____

d. Misha goes to school by car. (sometimes)

____

4. Fill in each blank with a **comparative** or **superlative adverb** formed from the adjective given in the brackets.

a. Let me explain the problem again ____________. (simple)

b. The metro will get us to our destination the ____________. (speedy)

c. Does the nightingale sing ____________ than the blackbird? (sweet)

d. Even the ____________ written comedy can fail. (clever)

5. Fill in each blank with a **comparative** or **superlative adverb** formed from the adverb given in the brackets.

a. Today I got up ____________ than usual. (early)

b. Of all age groups, elderly folk use the Internet the ____________. (little)

c. The next village was ____________ affected by the floods than ours was. (badly)

d. We arrived ____________ than we had expected to. (late)

e. The team have performed ____________ than last year. (well)

6. Combine each pair of sentences into a single sentence using a **comparative adverb**.

Example Dev ran 5 kilometres. Hari ran 6 kilometres.

Hari ran further than Dev.

a. Shashi swam a length in 16 seconds. Shanti swam a length in 17 seconds.

____

b. Ravi uses the gym a lot. Sadia doesn't use the gym much.

____

c. Gina cleared the pole at 1 metre. Sita cleared the pole at 1 metre 6 centimetres.

____

 ISBN 978-93-5103-603-6

6.2 Adverbs of degree

Read the story.

Charlie was **very** keen on making models. He showed Jack a **rather** complicated aeroplane he had made.

Jack **pretty** foolishly pushed it out of the window. Charlie was **terribly** upset.

Charlie **very** crossly explained that the models were only for display. Jack was **extremely** sorry.

What do you think happened to Charlie's aeroplane?

What had Charlie made?

How did Charlie feel when Jack pushed his aeroplane out of the window?

How did Jack feel later?

1. Note the highlighted words in the story above. Now circle the words that say something more about the underlined word in each sentence.

   a. Charlie was particularly pleased with his model aeroplane.

   b. He very proudly showed it to Jack.

   c. Jack was pretty silly not to realise the model was only for display.

   d. Charlie was extremely annoyed.

   e. Later, he explained things quite patiently to Jack.

2. Fill in each blank with a word from the box below that says something more about the adjective or adverb in the sentence.

very	really	fairly	quite	extremely

   a. You performed ________ well at the singing competition today.

   b. That's a ________ fine painting, isn't it?

   c. Break the eggs ________ carefully into the bowl.

   d. We had ________ good weather during our trip.

   e. There was ________ a large audience in the theatre.

Words such as **very**, **fairly**, **quite**, **pretty**, **rather**, **really**, **particularly**, **terribly** or **extremely** are used before an adjective or adverb to say "how much" or "to what extent". They are called **adverbs of degree**.

 ISBN 978-93-5103-603-6

Let's Practise

A. Underline the **adverb of degree** in each sentence.

1. You did fairly well in the test.
2. The children are being extremely quiet.
3. The rules are now quite different.
4. Things turned out terribly badly for Mrs Raman.
5. The concert was rather dull.
6. The Taj Mahal is really beautiful.

B. Rewrite each sentence, adding a suitable **adverb of degree** from the box below.

very	extremely	pretty	rather	terribly	quite

Example The sun is hot at midday.

The sun is very hot at midday.

1. The argument ended peacefully.

   ____

2. I was upset not to get a prize.

   ____

3. Jamshid carelessly left his car unlocked.

   ____

4. We would be delighted if you could join us.

   ____

5. Some secret documents have been stolen.

   ____

C. Fill in each blank with **too** and an **adjective** from the box below.

fast	late	high	tired	hot

1. It's ______________ for sitting in the sun.
2. I hope it's not ______________ to get the concert tickets?
3. I tried to go on working but I was ______________.
4. The thief ran ______________ for us to catch him.
5. The branch is ______________. I can't reach it.

Take Note

We use the adverb of degree **too** before an adjective or adverb if that adjective or adverb makes something seem impossible, e.g. The river's **too** fast for swimming.

 ISBN 978-93-5103-603-6

6.3 Interrogative adverbs

Remember!
Interrogative pronouns such as **who**, **whose**, **whom**, **what** or **which** are used in place of nouns. Interrogative adjectives such as **what**, **which** or **whose** are used before a noun.

Read the story.

"**How** was your holiday?" asked Anna. "Oh, it was amazing!" answered Sue.

"**When** did you get back?" asked Anna. "I got back yesterday," said Sue.

"**Where** did you go?" asked Anna. "I went to Rome and Florence!" replied Sue excitedly.

Do you think Sue enjoys travelling? Do you like travelling? Who do you travel with?

What did Anna ask Sue first?

What did she want to know next?

What was Anna's last question?

1. Note the highlighted words in the story above. Now use them to complete these questions.

   a. ________ did Sue go on her holiday?

   b. ________ did she get back from her holiday?

   c. ________ did she enjoy her holiday?

2. Form a question for each sentence below.

   a. ______________________________

   The keys are in the top drawer.

   b. ______________________________

   I'm going out because I need some fresh air.

   c. ______________________________

   I'll be home by six o'clock.

   d. ______________________________

   The dog got out by crawling under the gate.

The adverbs **where**, **when** and **how** ask about the place, time and manner of a happening or action. **Why** asks the reason for it. They are called **interrogative adverbs**.

 ISBN 978-93-5103-603-6

Let's Practise

A. Fill in each blank with **where**, **when**, **why** or **how**.

1. ________ could I have left my watch?
2. ________ did the thief get into the apartment?
3. ________ was the match cancelled?
4. ________ does the vacation start?

B. Use **how** and a word from the box below to complete each question.

far	much	old	many	expensive	long

1. ____________ is your sister?
2. ____________ does this mobile phone cost?
3. ____________ copies do you want?
4. ____________ did you have to wait?
5. ____________ did you walk?
6. ____________ is this watch?

Take Note

The adverb **how** can be used with

- adjectives, e.g. **How tall** are you?
- other adverbs, e.g. **How well** did Mala dance?
- **much** or **many**, e.g. **How much** money have you got? **How many** sisters do you have?

C. Form a question for each sentence using an **interrogative adverb**.

1. ______________________________

   The thieves escaped by breaking open the back door.

2. ______________________________

   She's upset because she just lost her job.

3. ______________________________

   They will land in Singapore around nine o'clock.

4. ______________________________

   Your spectacles are hanging round your neck!

5. ______________________________

   I am going to Istanbul in July.

Think & Share Pair up with a classmate to play detective. Ask your partner to describe a crime scene, such as a robbery. Ask questions about the crime using interrogative adverbs, for example, **How** did the robber get in? **Why** was the gate unlocked? Swap roles with your partner and continue the game.

 ISBN 978-93-5103-603-6

6.4 More about adverbs

Read the story.

How do you think Rufus escaped?

What did Granny tell Sam?

Did Rufus stay inside the gate?

What did Granny say when she saw Rufus outside?

1. Note the highlighted words in the story above. Now use them to fill in the blanks.

   a. Rufus was ____________ permitted to go out on the road.

   b. Granny did ____________ realise Rufus could jump over the fence.

   c. Rufus did ____________ obey any rules.

   d. He ____________ wasn't an obedient dog!

2. Fill in each blank with a suitable adverb from the box below.

not	nowhere	certainly	surely

   a. Please do ____________ lean bicycles against this wall.

   b. ____________ you want to get good marks in your exams?

   c. "Where have you been?" "____________ interesting."

   d. "Do you agree with me?" "I ____________ do!"

Adverbs such as **not** and **nowhere** are negative adverbs. Adverbs such as **certainly** and **surely** are used to strengthen a statement.

 ISBN 978-93-5103-603-6

Let's Practise

A. Rewrite each sentence given below as a negative sentence using the adverb **not**. Use the short form **-n't** where possible.

Example I have had a shower.

I haven't had a shower.

1. We have had our breakfast.

____

2. We must run across the road.

____

3. Tim has lost his watch.

____

4. Carol was sitting at her desk.

____

5. I shall wait for you.

____

6. I can remember her name.

____

7. Did you book the tickets?

____

8. I could hear her voice clearly.

____

B. Fill in each blank with a suitable **adverb** from the box below. You may use some adverbs more than once.

absolutely	definitely	surely	certainly

1. You may ________ join us for dinner.
2. I shall ________ come to the school to pick you up.
3. If you work hard, you will ________ do well in your exam.
4. I ________ agree with what you say.
5. "May I borrow your pen for a minute?" "________ you may."
6. ________ they'll lend us some money?
7. We can ________ go to the party.
8. They ________ don't need an invitation to visit us!

Take Note

- We use **surely** or **certainly** when we believe something to be true and expect others to agree with us.
- The adverbs **yes** or **no** can be used on their own to give a brief reply to a question, e.g. "Have you done your homework?" "**No**." "Have you had your breakfast?" "**Yes**."

 ISBN 978-93-5103-603-6

6.5 Adverb phrases

Read the story.

At seven o'clock the teenagers started arriving **at the dance hall.**

As the band struck up **on the stage**, everyone danced **with great energy.**

The noise could be heard **around the neighbourhood** and many of the residents were unable to sleep **that night**.

Remember!
A group of words that has meaning but does not make complete sense is called a phrase.

What do you think the residents will do about the noise?

When did the teenagers start arriving?

How did everyone dance?

Where could the noise be heard?

1. Note the highlighted phrases in the story above. Now circle the phrase that tells you something about the underlined verb in each sentence.
   a. The dance hall opened before seven o'clock.
   b. The band arrived on the stage and everyone cheered.
   c. Jenny tossed from side to side as she tried to sleep.

2. Fill in the blanks in the story with phrases from the box that tell you something about the action.

at last	right overhead	down the hill
because of my heavy load		down to the shops

Yesterday, I decided to go ________________ to buy some groceries.

The sun was shining ________________ as I walked ________________.

On the way back, I felt tired ________________. I was glad to get home

________________.

A phrase that plays the role of an adverb in a sentence is called an **adverb phrase**.

 ISBN 978-93-5103-603-6

Let's Practise

A. Complete each sentence with a suitable **adverb phrase** from the box below.

on the table	at ten-thirty	in complete silence
on to the boundary wall	in a hurry	at the hospital
across the sky	because of his positive attitude	

1. White clouds were racing ____________________.
2. I want all students to gather ____________________.
3. The cat jumped up ____________________.
4. Mum works ____________________.
5. Never make decisions ____________________.
6. The students listened ____________________.
7. He was promoted ____________________.
8. Dad unfolded his newspaper ____________________.

B. Underline the **adverb phrases** in the passage below.

Would you like to join me for dinner at the Blue Peacock Restaurant tomorrow? I know we went to the Pink Lotus last time, but I thought the food was not cooked to the best standard, and the waiter served us without much friendliness. My nephew is working as a waiter at the Blue Peacock, and we will get good service there! If you agree, I'll book a table for eight o'clock. Tomorrow morning I'll be at a meeting in Mumbai, but you can contact me on my mobile phone.

C. Match the columns to show what each underlined **adverb phrase** expresses.

1. They moved house because of the baby.	a. place
2. I met Mia last week.	b. manner
3. Hang your coats on the hooks provided.	c. time
4. She always greets everyone with a smile.	d. direction
5. We're flying to Paris.	e. reason

Think & Share Play a sorting game with your classmates. Label five boxes Place, Time, Manner, Direction and Reason. Write twenty sentences with adverb phrases on slips of paper and place them in a bowl. Each student has to pick a slip, identify the type of adverb phrase and drop it in the correct box.

Take Note
Adverb phrases often start with a preposition. An adverb phrase can tell us about
- the place of an action, e.g. You can get this book **in any bookstall**.
- the direction of an action, e.g. Sally is going **to school**.
- the time of an action, e.g. I watched a film **last night**.
- the manner of an action, e.g. The stone landed **with a thud**.
- the reason for an action, e.g. He was punished **because of his bad behaviour**.

 ISBN 978-93-5103-603-6

Review 2

1. Fill in each blank with a suitable **adjective of quantity** from the box below.

little	all	a little	few	a few	half	enough	five

a. I think we have ____________ players for a match.

b. We have many applicants but ____________ places.

c. The recipe requires ____________ teaspoons of sugar.

d. Could I have ____________ milk in my tea?

e. There are ____________ points to consider before we decide.

f. It will take ____________ an hour to cook dinner.

g. The air is so polluted that very ____________ sun gets through.

h. In spring flowers bloom on ____________ the trees.

2. Circle the correct **interrogative adjective** to complete each sentence.

a. (What / Which) road should I take to reach the stadium?

b. (What / Which) kind of fabric do you want for your dress?

c. (Whose / Which) lunch box have you taken by mistake?

d. (Which / Whose) novel from the collection did you enjoy the best?

e. (Which / Whose) exam was the hardest for you?

3. Make a sentence of your own with each **emphasising adjective**.

a. total ____________________

b. absolute ____________________

c. entire ____________________

d. utter ____________________

4. Underline the **adjective phrase** in each sentence.

a. The boy sitting in the corner is lost.

b. Screaming loudly, she jumped up from her chair.

c. A bus filled with excited children has just arrived.

d. The man in the seat next to Mum is my gym teacher.

e. The ambulance slowly made its way through the heavily crowded street.

 ISBN 978-93-5103-603-6

5. Circle the **verb** in each sentence. In the brackets, write **T** if it is transitive or **I** if it is intransitive.

a. Usha was combing her hair. [ ]
b. Aren't you going to school today? [ ]
c. Aisha has a job in the supermarket. [ ]
d. Mum ran warm water into the bath. [ ]
e. It rained all day. [ ]
f. Ajit plays the trumpet in the orchestra. [ ]
g. Did you see the helicopter? [ ]
h. The cricket match was very exciting. [ ]

Remember!
To test if a verb is transitive or intransitive, we can ask "What?" or "Whom?" after saying the verb. If there is no answer, the verb is intransitive.

6. Underline the **direct object** in each sentence. Then circle the **indirect object**, if any.

a. I'll leave a meal for you, ready to microwave.
b. Sheela made her mother a beautiful birthday card.
c. Mr Lal donated a lot of money to the school.
d. Mum sang the baby a lullaby.
e. Every day we read our teacher a few lines of the story.
f. Send me a letter when you're abroad.
g. Priya cooked pasta for dinner.
h. Zara told Arish a story.

7. Circle the **incomplete verb** and underline the **complement** in each sentence.

a. Dilip seems a nice boy.
b. Arun's project sounded very exciting.
c. The eclipse turned the sky completely dark.
d. The people in the flat above are Armenian.
e. The Board of School Governors elected Hamid chairman.
f. Sanjay wants to become a businessman.

8. Match the underlined words with their grammatical names on the right.

a. Rain stopped <u>play</u>.	•	• i. indirect object
b. Dev <u>trained</u> in London.	•	• ii. complement
c. They declared Shanti <u>the winner</u>.	•	• iii. intransitive verb
d. Hema <u>drives</u> a van.	•	• iv. direct object
e. We awarded <u>Jay</u> first prize.	•	• v. transitive verb

 ISBN 978-93-5103-603-6

9. Fill in each blank with the **present** or **past participle** of a verb from the box below. Then underline the whole **participle phrase**.

read	kill	compose	leave	scare	write	stand	sit

a. The monument honours the soldiers ________ in the war.
b. ________ in very small letters, the address was hard to read.
c. Do you see those people ________ on the bench?
d. ________ by the noise, the baby started crying.
e. He sat in a corner of the carriage, ________ a newspaper.
f. Music ________ by Mozart is always recognisable.
g. I didn't notice Rajiv ________ the hall.
h. Fortunately no one ________ on the platform was injured.

10. Look at the underlined word in each sentence. In the brackets, write **G** if it is a gerund or **P** if it is a participle.

a. Learning a musical instrument will be good for you. [ ]
b. Typing busily at her keyboard, Sara failed to notice the time. [ ]
c. Though quite musical, Javed didn't enjoy practising the piano. [ ]
d. Reading is a good habit. [ ]
e. I stood still, listening to the strange noise. [ ]
f. There's no point in regretting the past. [ ]
g. The growing crowd listened intently to the speaker. [ ]
h. Training with Zahir made Sunil a good athlete. [ ]

11. Fill in each blank with a suitable **adverb of degree** from the box below.

fairly	too	pretty	highly	a little	extremely	quite	rather

a. If you got all the answers correct you did ________ well.
b. We can climb a bit higher if you're not ________ tired.
c. The weather was ________ good, with lots of sun and a few showers.
d. Sue has a mischievous smile that is ________ attractive.
e. You all sang well. It has been ________ difficult to choose a winner.
f. Please take precautions as the disease is ________ contagious.
g. I think your explanation is ________ inaccurate.
h. Think carefully, and you'll solve the puzzle ________ easily.

 ISBN 978-93-5103-603-6

12. Fill in each blank with a suitable **interrogative adverb**.

a. ________ did they get through a locked door?

b. ________ have I left my jacket?

c. ________ are you looking so puzzled?

d. ________ does the play start?

13. Fill in each blank with a suitable **adverb** from the box below. You may use some adverbs more than once.

certainly	definitely	not	absolutely	nowhere	surely

a. I looked for that photo but it was ________ to be found.

b. You may ________ take your calculator into the exam room.

c. ________ he knows it's dangerous to drive a motorcycle without a helmet?

d. You may ________ come with us to the exhibition.

e. These allegations are ________ false!

f. I'll ________ attend the meeting.

g. The tools Rahul gave me are ________ useless.

h. Sid may ________ participate in the race tomorrow.

14. Underline the **adverb phrases** in the story.

Last night I set my alarm clock to go off at 5.30 a.m. I was in the land of dreams when the alarm rang this morning. Reluctantly I climbed out of bed, had a quick shower in the bathroom, got dressed in my travel clothes, collected my backpack from the hallway, and walked to the station at a brisk pace. The lady standing at the ticket barrier let me on to the platform with a cheerful smile, and I settled myself in the right seat, in the right carriage.

Spot the Error

15. There is a mistake in each sentence. Underline it and rewrite the passage correctly in your notebook.

Sheela was terrifically upset. "There isn't no olive oil, and there are no vegetables either," she complained. "Why can I cook a meal with no vegetables? Which turn was it to buy vegetables this week? And there you are, all sitting in a row watching television, expected a fancy meal. Is anyone interesting in helping us? Talking to you all is a whole waste of time."

 ISBN 978-93-5103-603-6

7 Prepositions

Let's Recall

- **Prepositions** show a connection between people and things.
- A preposition that tells us the position of one thing or person in relation to another is called a **preposition of place**.
- A preposition that connects a happening with a point in time to tell us when something happens is called a **preposition of time**.

7.1 Revising prepositions

1. Fill in each blank with a suitable **preposition of place** or **time** from the box below.

down	for	besides	around	since	beside
to	in	before	during	on	

a. There was a little table ________ the bed.

b. I've several other chores to do ________ the ironing.

c. Our neighbours have just built a fence ________ their house.

d. We walked ________ the steps ________ the beach.

e. My parents have been married ________ thirty years.

f. Read the instructions ________ using the oven.

g. The college library is closed ________ the vacation.

h. You must complete the test ________ twenty minutes.

i. I'm going to the doctor ________ Monday.

j. I have known Alisha ________ my early childhood.

Take Note

- You use **since** to specify the beginning of a period of time, e.g. I have been waiting for you **since** 3 p.m.
- You use **for** to specify the length of a period of time, e.g. I have waited for you **for** two hours.

2. Look at the underlined word in each sentence. In the brackets, write **P** if it is a preposition or **A** if it is an adverb.

a. The Menon family live <u>up</u> on the top floor. [ ]

b. The festival's over. It's time to take <u>down</u> the decorations. [ ]

c. We had a great time sliding <u>down</u> the chute. [ ]

d. I watched the spider crawling <u>up</u> the wall. [ ]

 ISBN 978-93-5103-603-6

7.2 More about prepositions

Read the story.

At seven minutes past eight a lot of people are waiting to get **onto** the train, including Mr Grey.

As the train speeds **along** the track, many passengers have to hold **onto** straps or seats **until** the stop where they get **off** the train.

The return train is emptier **than** the morning one. Mr Grey sits down and places his briefcase **upon** his knees.

Why do you think the train is so busy in the morning?

Why are the people waiting?

How long do the passengers hold onto straps and seats?

How is the return train different from the morning one?

1. Fill in each blank with a highlighted preposition from the story above.

   a. The trains are busy ____________ mid-morning.

   b. Standing passengers have to hold ____________ something.

   c. Mr Grey's return train was less busy ____________ his morning one.

   d. The train speeded ____________ the tracks.

   e. Mr Grey got ____________ the train and caught a bus.

2. Match the columns to make complete sentences.

a. Steve will play	•	•	i. round the fire and told stories.
b. We sat	•	•	ii. opposite my school.
c. Is it time to get	•	•	iii. upon your actions.
d. My house is	•	•	iv. off the bus?
e. The result will depend	•	•	v. against Danny in the final.

The prepositions **along**, **onto**, **off**, **upon**, **round**, **against** and **opposite** are often used to show the physical relationship between things or people. **Than** is used to make comparisons. **Until** can be a preposition of place or time.

 ISBN 978-93-5103-603-6

Let's Practise

A. Circle the correct **preposition** to complete each sentence.

1. She stood with her back (upon / against) the door.
2. We had to wait (until / before) the interval to buy an ice cream.
3. Remo and Aditi were sitting (opposite / against) each other.
4. This route is slightly shorter (from / than) our usual one.
5. We walked (round / about) the statue, looking up at it.

B. Fill in each blank with a suitable **preposition** from the box below.

along	off	upon	onto	against	than

1. Let me ask you a question ________ another subject.
2. The pictures look good ________ the dark wall.
3. Choose any number greater ________ six.
4. I knocked the ornament ________ the shelf.
5. Make sure you get ________ the right train.
6. Walk ________ that path and you'll reach the lake.

C. Look at the underlined word in each sentence. In the brackets, write **P** if it is a preposition or **A** if it is an adverb.

1. It's dangerous to walk <u>along</u> the wall. [ ]
2. You might fall <u>off</u>. [ ]
3. I haven't been here before. Could you show me <u>round</u>? [ ]
4. That wall isn't strong enough to lean the ladder <u>against</u>. [ ]
5. The houses standing <u>opposite</u> are to be pulled down. [ ]

Think & Share Get into groups and play a game of Dumb Charades with prepositions. Each group prepares a list of prepositions, such as **opposite**, **against**, **along**, **upon**, **onto** and acts out situations describing them. The other groups must try and guess what these prepositions are.

Take Note

- **Onto** is often written as **on to**.
- **Upon** is an alternative to **on**. It can also mean "about", e.g. He wrote **upon** various subjects.
- **Until** is usually used as a preposition of time, e.g. I waited **until** daybreak. Sometimes it is used as a preposition of place, e.g. Stay on the train **until** the third stop.
- **Round** is an alternative to **around**, e.g. He showed me **round**/**around** the museum.
- Sometimes, the object of the preposition may come before it, e.g. That is the lady he was chatting **with**. What is this switch **for**?

Take Note

A preposition requires an object. An adverb has no object.

 ISBN 978-93-5103-603-6

7.3 Complex prepositions

Read the story.

Old Mr Thomas walked **down to** the lake very slowly **because of** his sore back.

He decided to have a rest **rather than** a long walk. **In front of** him was a peaceful scene of sailing boats.

Later on, he climbed the steps **up to** the road. The bus stop was **close to** the steps.

What do you think Mr Thomas did next?

Why did he walk slowly?

What did he decide?

What did he do later on?

1. Note the highlighted prepositions in the story above. Now underline the group of words that acts as a preposition in each sentence.
   a. In front of Mr Thomas lay a pretty lake.
   b. He always used a walking stick because of his bad back.
   c. There was a narrow path leading down to the lake.
   d. There was a railing all around the lake.

2. Fill in each blank with a suitable preposition from the box below.

next to	in spite of	due to	on top of	out of	along with

   a. We keep vases ____________ the kitchen cupboard.
   b. Come ____________ me to the party.
   c. The delay was ____________ a broken signal.
   d. Who do you want to sit ____________?
   e. I took the cake ____________ the oven.
   f. He decided to go to work ____________ the heavy rain.

Take Note
A preposition that is made up of only one word is a **simple preposition**.

A preposition that is made up of more than one word is called a **complex preposition**.

 ISBN 978-93-5103-603-6

Let's Practise

A. Underline the **complex preposition** in each sentence.

1. I want to study Physics rather than Maths.
2. I'll walk with you up to the fountain.
3. They got out of the bus to stretch their legs.
4. Vicky is sitting next to Asha.
5. My cousins live close to the airport.

B. Fill in each blank with the correct **complex preposition** from the box below.

due to	on top of	in front of
along with	down to	up to

1. Vishal's sore throat was ________ an infection.
2. It's quite scary standing ________ an audience.
3. I went ________ Sara to the party.
4. There is a huge telescope ________ the observatory.
5. Nazir walked ________ the shop at the end of the street.
6. A man came ________ me and asked the time.

C. Fill in the blanks in the story with suitable **complex prepositions** from the box below.

in front of	out of	up to	down to
in spite of	because of	close to	

I came ____________ the house at eight o'clock and walked ____________ the metro station. I went ____________ the ticket counter. Many people were standing in the queue ____________ me. In summer, people prefer the metro ____________ the heat outside. ____________ the rush, I reached my destination in good time. Luckily, my office is ____________ the metro station.

Think & Share Pair up with a classmate to play the preposition game. Select a picture and describe it to your partner without letting them see it. Use complex prepositions such as **in front of**, **next to** and **on top of** in your description. Your partner has to draw on a sheet of paper whatever you describe. When the drawing is complete, compare it with your picture. How accurate was your description?

 ISBN 978-93-5103-603-6

8 Conjunctions

Let's Recall

- Conjunctions are words that help to join words, phrases or sentences together.
- Conjunctions such as **and** and **as well as** are usually used to link ideas that are similar in sense or that go together. The conjunctions **or**, **although**, **unless** and **but** often introduce an opposite idea. Conjunctions such as **because** and **so** deal with the reason for something.

8.1 Revising conjunctions

1. Circle the correct **conjunction** to complete each sentence.

a. We didn't know whether to turn right (or / but) go straight on.

b. The weather was very sunny (but / so) rather windy.

c. Mark's visit was very welcome, (or / though) it was quite unexpected.

d. The children visited Disneyland (but / and) thoroughly enjoyed it.

e. The hill was steep and rocky, (so / though) quite difficult to climb.

f. We couldn't go paragliding (unless / since) there wasn't enough wind.

g. Rohini said she'll be back by eight o'clock (unless / as soon as) there was a lot of traffic.

h. Now that I can drive, I can leave the house (as long as / whenever) I want to!

2. Fill in each blank with a suitable **conjunction** from the box below.

although	while	because	when	if	until

a. Everyone goes to the seaside __________ summer comes.

b. __________ it rains, the party will be held indoors.

c. James was a very responsible boy, __________ he was only ten.

d. They went on talking on the veranda __________ it was dark.

e. I lay on the grass __________ the birds sang in the trees.

f. Jay wasn't allowed into the cinema __________ he was too young.

 ISBN 978-93-5103-603-6

8.2 More about conjunctions

Read the story.

When Rosa reached the station she was **both** tired **and** hungry. She handed over her ticket quickly.

"Your train left five minutes ago," said the ticket collector. **Neither** he **nor** Rosa looked happy!

"You can **either** catch the next train **or** take the faster one from the next platform," he suggested.

What do you think Rosa will do?

How did she feel when she reached the station?

Who did not look happy?

What did the ticket collector then suggest?

1. Note the highlighted pairs of words in the story above. Now use them to fill in the blanks in each sentence.

   a. Rosa had ________ breakfast ________ lunch on Monday, so she was very hungry.

   b. She decided to have ________ a sandwich ________ a burger.

   c. "I can take ________ an apple juice ________ a cola with it," she thought.

2. Rewrite each pair of sentences as one sentence. The words in the brackets will help you.

   Example Rajiv doesn't enjoy gym. Rajiv doesn't enjoy dancing.
   Rajiv enjoys neither gym nor dancing.

   a. The metro is fast. It is also punctual. (both/and)

   ____

   b. You can play cricket. You can play tennis. (either/or)

   ____

   c. Tejas can speak Spanish. Tejas can speak French. (not only/but also)

   ____

Paired words such as **either…or**, **neither…nor**, **not only…but also** and **both…and** are also **conjunctions**.

 ISBN 978-93-5103-603-6

Let's Practise

A. Underline the **pair of conjunctions** in each sentence.

1. Dad decided to buy not only the red shirt but also the grey one.
2. We were going neither to the park nor to the cinema. We were going to Space Museum!
3. You can either sit alone and be bored or join everyone and have fun.
4. Both Sam and Sally will attend Hillside School.
5. Aman drinks neither tea nor coffee.

B. Fill in the blanks with the correct **pair of conjunctions** from the box below.

not only...but also	neither...nor	either...or	both...and

1. Harish ________ wrote to me ________ telephoned me.
2. ________ the fridge isn't working ________ someone has turned it off by mistake.
3. Gita ________ sings well ________ plays the piano.
4. ________ Rahul ________ his wife play golf very well.

C. Rewrite each sentence using the **pair of conjunctions** given in the brackets.

Example Rahim is a brilliant scientist and a good poet. (not only...but also)

Rahim is not only a brilliant scientist but also a good poet.

1. Usha didn't enjoy sport and she didn't enjoy indoor games. (neither...nor)

____

2. Zubaida has forgotten the meeting or I've got the time wrong. (either...or)

____

3. The house has a big front lawn and a huge backyard. (both...and)

____

Think & Share Pair up with a classmate and make a list of conjunctions that appear in pairs. Then start a sentence using the first of a pair of conjunctions and ask your partner to complete the sentence using the second conjunction of the pair.

 ISBN 978-93-5103-603-6

9 Sentences

Let's Recall

- A **sentence** is a group of words that makes complete sense. It is divided into **subject** and **predicate**. The predicate contains the verb.
- A verb must **agree** with its subject. A singular subject has a singular verb and a plural subject has a plural verb.
- A **phrase** is a group of words that has meaning but does not make complete sense. It does not have a subject or predicate.
- A sentence that makes a statement is an **assertive** or **declarative sentence**. A sentence that makes a negative statement, using **not** or **never**, is a **negative sentence**. A sentence that asks a question and ends with a question mark is an **interrogative sentence**. A sentence that expresses a strong feeling and ends with an exclamation mark is an **exclamatory sentence**. A sentence that gives an order or command is an **imperative sentence**.

9.1 Revising sentences

1. Circle the **subject** and underline the **predicate** in each sentence.
   a. Jamal and Jahan have sold their house.
   b. I'm not used to such rudeness.
   c. The secretary at the British Embassy gave us a form to complete.
   d. Who left the gate into the field open?
   e. Hang your coat on that peg.
   f. Suddenly, out of the front door ran a man carrying a sack.
   g. Nowhere else do you see such amazing birds.
   h. Please be careful!

Take Note
Sometimes the subject is not mentioned in the sentence. This is common in imperative sentences, e.g. Sit down. Please wash your hands. (The subject **You** is not mentioned here, but it is understood or implied.)

2. Match the **subjects** with the **predicates** to make complete sentences.

a. The garden •	• i. reads me a story at bedtime.
b. Dad •	• ii. clapped enthusiastically.
c. The dentist •	• iii. begins at eight o'clock.
d. The play •	• iv. examined my teeth thoroughly.
e. The audience •	• v. is my elder brother.
f. Naseer •	• vi. looks beautiful this morning.

 ISBN 978-93-5103-603-6

3. Circle the **verb** that agrees with the **subject** to complete each sentence.

a. Your luggage (are / is) waiting in the hallway.

b. The band (was / were) packing away their instruments.

c. Everyone (wishes / wish) you a good journey.

d. People (thinks / think) differently on this subject.

e. Four hundred grams of sugar (is / are) enough for this recipe.

f. Kanti and Shashi (goes / go) to the same school.

g. A comedian is happy when the audience all (laughs / laugh).

h. The team (has / have) had its problems.

4. Fill in each blank with the correct singular or plural present tense of the **verb** given in the brackets.

a. The news about the war __________ me. (worry)

b. The cattle __________ peacefully in the summer sunshine. (graze)

c. Measles __________ a certain number of children each year. (kill)

d. Who usually __________ up the shop? (lock)

e. The police __________ every incident reported to them by the public. (investigate)

f. One of my friends __________ professionally. (dance)

g. Each family __________ its own routines. (create)

h. The clothes __________ stacked in a pile. (be)

5. Fill in the blanks in the story with **verbs** that agree with the **subjects**.

Yesterday Mum, Dad, Priya and I __________ just sitting down in the kitchen for our evening meal when there __________ a knock at the door. It __________ Arun and Sita from next door. The two of them __________ wanting to play with Priya and me. Mum said, "I'm afraid our family __________ just taken their places at the table and __________ having their dinner. Why __________ you two go into the living room and wait for twenty minutes or so? There __________ a stack of DVDs over in the corner. One of those __________ sure to interest you. You can sit on the sofa and watch it till Dilip and Priya __________ free to play with you."

 ISBN 978-93-5103-603-6

6. Look at each group of words. In the brackets, write **S** if it is a sentence or **P** if it is a phrase.

a. A thoroughly enjoyable evening [ ]

b. It was an unexpected treat [ ]

c. Will have been working [ ]

d. Down by the riverside [ ]

e. Round the bend came a lorry [ ]

f. Standing behind me in the queue [ ]

g. Into the bin with all this rubbish [ ]

h. Dressed in a clown outfit [ ]

Remember!
Unlike a sentence, a phrase does not make complete sense.

7. Expand each **phrase** into a **sentence** of your own.

a. on the right path

____

b. two pupils from this school

____

c. must have been joking

____

d. right through the window

____

e. freshly mown

____

f. my pet parrot

____

8. Look at each sentence. In the brackets, write **A** for assertive, **N** for negative, **I** for interrogative, **E** for exclamatory or **Im** for imperative.

a. Please stop switching TV channels. [ ]

b. I have done nothing to be punished for. [ ]

c. What will you wear for the prize-giving? [ ]

d. What a nuisance these roadworks are! [ ]

e. People should be more careful of the environment. [ ]

f. Never take no for an answer. [ ]

g. This is the most boring film I have ever seen! [ ]

h. Sam does not like going to the amusement arcade. [ ]

i. When will Dad return from Spain? [ ]

 ISBN 978-93-5103-603-6

9. Change each **assertive sentence** into a **negative sentence**. Use short forms where possible.

Example I have finished my homework.

I haven't finished my homework.

a. Meena had forgotten to pass on the message.

____

b. My parents were impressed by the school concert.

____

c. It is the first time this has happened.

____

d. Keeping a pet means a lot of extra work.

____

10. Change each **assertive sentence** into an **exclamatory sentence**.

Example The weather is lovely.

How lovely the weather is!

Take Note
Exclamatory sentences can have an incomplete structure, e.g. **How amazing!**

a. Those clouds look weird.

____

b. The children's play was a delightful production.

____

c. That talk was interesting.

____

d. Some people lead exciting lives.

____

11. Answer each **interrogative sentence** with an **assertive sentence**. Begin with **Yes**.

Example Were you at home yesterday?

Yes, I was at home yesterday.

a. Can we discuss this later?

____

b. Should we inform the police?

____

c. Will the timetable remain the same?

____

d. Did you see the balloon?

____

 ISBN 978-93-5103-603-6

9.2 Clauses

Read the story.

It was Uma's birthday and **she was opening her presents**.

When **Uma opened her brother Jay's present, she found** that **he had given her a DVD**.

In the evening they all went to a restaurant and **were welcomed by the manager**.

Do you think Uma had a good time at the restaurant?

Why had Uma received presents?

What was Jay's present to Uma?

What did they do in the evening?

1. Note the highlighted groups of words in the story above. Now underline the groups of words in each sentence that have a subject and a verb.
   a. It was Uma's birthday and she had received lots of gifts.
   b. Mum, Dad and Jay had their breakfast while she unwrapped the gifts.
   c. Uma was happy that Jay had given her a great DVD.
   d. Dad had booked a table at a restaurant so that they could celebrate Uma's birthday.
   e. The manager welcomed them warmly because he knew them well.

2. Underline the groups of words that have a subject and a verb. Then circle the conjunction that joins them in each sentence.
   a. Sara went home early because she felt sick.
   b. The lady at the post office told me that the price of stamps was going up.
   c. You should always lock the door when you go out.
   d. How you've grown since you started school!
   e. The document will not be valid unless you sign it.

A group of words that has a subject and a verb is called a **clause**. A clause may form a sentence on its own or it may form part of a sentence.

 ISBN 978-93-5103-603-6

Let's Practise

A. Join the two **clauses** in each sentence using a suitable conjunction from the box below.

if	but	because	until	before	although

1. Gita was ill yesterday __________ she's better today.
2. I always brush my teeth __________ I go to bed.
3. You will have to work hard __________ you want to go to university.
4. Rajiv must stay away from school __________ his spots disappear.
5. We cancelled the match __________ so many players were ill.
6. They decided to go walking in the hills __________ the forecast was bad.

B. Circle the **subjects** and underline the **verbs**. In the brackets, write how many **clauses** each sentence has.

Example The farmer gets up when the sun rises and he works in the fields until the sun sets. [4]

1. You shouldn't count your chickens until they are hatched. [ ]
2. Mum was anxious because Dad was late, so she was relieved when he arrived home. [ ]
3. When Abhijeet was travelling he visited the village where he was born. [ ]
4. We couldn't understand why the train had stopped. [ ]
5. Sita picked out the books that she no longer needed and she sold them. [ ]
6. We should book tickets now or it will be too late. [ ]

Take Note

A sentence may have

- only one clause, e.g. We often feed the birds in the park.
- two clauses linked by a conjunction, e.g. We often feed the birds **and** we sometimes go on the swings in the park.
- more than two clauses, e.g. We often feed the birds **and** we sometimes go on the swings **when** we go to the park.

C. Read each **clause** and circle the **conjunction**. Then add another clause to complete the sentence.

1. When you visit Grandmother ______________________________
2. Although Leela was only ten ______________________________
3. While Dad put the children to bed ______________________________.
4. Since you were last here ______________________________.
5. Wherever we went ______________________________.
6. As it was getting late ______________________________.

 ISBN 978-93-5103-603-6

9.3 Coordinate clauses

Read the story.

Mrs Green's pupils made a map of the town, and **they drew pictures of well-known buildings to stick on it.**

Peter and Sally each drew a church, so **Mrs Green stuck their drawings on the map in the right positions.**

Rita made a picture of a hospital, but **Eddie made a picture of their own school to stick on the map.**

What other well-known buildings would you find in a town?

What did Mrs Green's pupils do?

What did Peter and Sally draw?

What did Eddie make?

1. Note the highlighted clauses in the story above. Now underline both the clauses in each sentence and circle the conjunction that joins them.
   a. Peter drew one church and Sally drew another.
   b. Is the school north of the river, or is it south of it?
   c. Mrs Green liked all the drawings, but she liked Eddie's the best.
   d. The finished map looked very nice, so everyone was pleased.

2. Underline the two clauses in each sentence. Then rewrite it as two sentences.

   Example Dilip came into the room and he took off his coat.
   Dilip came into the room. He took off his coat.

   a. Sita and Usha went to the play but they didn't enjoy it.

   ____

   b. I may walk to school or I may take the bus.

   ____

   c. The weather is bright and sunny, so it is quite pleasant.

   ____

Clauses linked by the conjunctions **and**, **but**, **or** and **so** are called **coordinate clauses**. These clauses are independent clauses that make complete sense on their own.

 ISBN 978-93-5103-603-6

Let's Practise

A. Underline the two **coordinate clauses** in each sentence. Then rewrite it as two sentences.

1. It was getting late, so I decided to take a taxi.

   ____

2. Sanjay is a good student and doesn't mind hard work.

   ____

3. The book was not well written but I quite enjoyed the story.

   ____

4. The Naiks have either gone out or can't hear the doorbell.

   ____

5. Dev failed his driving test so had to take it again.

   ____

Take Note

- The conjunctions linking coordinate clauses are called coordinating conjunctions.
- If the subject of both clauses is the same person, animal or thing, we can omit the subject from the second clause.

B. Add a suitable conjunction to join the two **coordinate clauses** in each sentence.

1. Indu failed her Maths exam __________ she didn't care.
2. Choose a drink __________ help yourself to some food.
3. Take a seat __________ stand if you prefer.
4. There was no reason to hope __________ we went on hoping.
5. Salim had a sore throat __________ he couldn't go swimming.

C. Use each pair of sentences and the conjunction given in the brackets to make a sentence with **coordinate clauses**. Omit the subject from the second clause, if it is not required.

1. We expected the weather to be good. It rained all the time. (but)

   ____

2. Arun takes a packed lunch. He buys food from a street vendor. (or)

   ____

3. Sara got excellent marks in the exam. She was delighted. (so)

   ____

4. Deepak picked some roses. He took them to his grandmother. (and)

   ____

5. Moin wants to buy a pair of jeans. The shops are all closed. (but)

   ____

 ISBN 978-93-5103-603-6

9.4 Subordinate clauses

Read the story.

Mark practises playing the trumpet with the school's band **when lessons are over**.

As soon as he gets home, he practises the trumpet again in his bedroom.

Mark's parents take him to a band competition. He watches the bands **as they get out of their buses**.

Remember!

- A group of words that has a subject and a verb is called a clause.
- Conjunctions can consist of more than one word.

Do you think Mark enjoyed the competition?

When does Mark practise the trumpet?

When does he practise it again?

What does he see at the competition?

1. Note the highlighted clauses in the story above. Now underline both the clauses in each sentence and circle the conjunction that joins them.
   a. The school brass band held rehearsals when lessons were over.
   b. Mark practised the trumpet as soon as he got home every day.
   c. His parents were so pleased that they took Mark to a band competition.
   d. Mark wants to join a big band when he turns fifteen.
2. Circle the conjunction and underline the clause that goes with it in each sentence. Then double-underline the clause that makes complete sense by itself.
   a. They will have the reception outdoors unless it rains.
   b. You interrupted before I'd finished speaking.
   c. After you've done your reading, you may go home.
   d. We took Mum to the doctor because she was ill.
   e. Although she has a licence, Swati does not drive.

In a sentence, the clause that makes complete sense by itself is the **main** or **principal clause**. A clause that doesn't make sense on its own and depends for its sense on the main clause is called a **subordinate** or **dependent clause**.

 ISBN 978-93-5103-603-6

Let's Practise

A. Complete each sentence with a suitable **subordinate clause** from the box below.

as soon as it stopped raining	unless it's a real emergency	until you return
since she was a little girl	before you make your weekend plans	

1. I'll wait here ______________________________.
2. ______________________________, Aisha has always wanted to dance.
3. Check the weather forecast ______________________________.
4. Don't dial the emergency number ______________________________.
5. ______________________________, I went out to play tennis.

B. Rewrite each sentence with the **subordinate clause** at the end.

Example After the market shuts down, the street is deserted.
The street is deserted after the market shuts down.

1. Before you set off, check your route on the map.
____
2. Since I last saw you, you've grown a beard.
____
3. As it's the last day of term, you can go home early.
____
4. When I go to bed, I switch off all the lights.
____

Take Note
- A subordinate clause can be placed at the beginning or end of a sentence.
- Subordinate clauses are introduced by conjunctions such as **when**, **if**, **because**, **unless** and **as soon as**. These are called subordinating conjunctions.

C. Circle the conjunction after each main clause given below. Then complete the sentence with a **subordinate clause** of your own.

1. The roof leaks whenever ______________________________.
2. She got a special prize because ______________________________.
3. I'm so hungry that ______________________________.
4. Take all your belongings with you when ______________________________.
5. Asha has had her hair cut short since ______________________________.
6. You may borrow the money from me as long as ______________________________.
7. Sit down and eat your nice hot meal before ______________________________.
8. We shall amuse ourselves until ______________________________.

 ISBN 978-93-5103-603-6

9.5 Noun clauses

Read the story.

David felt hot and decided **that he needed a swim in the river**.

He thought **how peaceful everything seemed under the water**.

He didn't realise **that the wind had blown his neatly folded T-shirt and shorts into the river**!

What do you think David did next?

What did David decide when he felt hot?

What were his thoughts while swimming?

What didn't he realise?

1. Note the highlighted clauses in the story above. Now underline the clause that is the object of the underlined verb in each sentence.

   a. It was a hot day and David thought that a swim would be very pleasant.

   b. People often say how peaceful it is to swim underwater.

   c. David didn't notice that it was rather windy.

   d. He saw that his clothes were floating in the water!

   e. He realised too late that he should have weighted them down with a stone.

Take Note

The clause that tells you what someone says or thinks is the object of the saying or thinking verb.

2. Match the clauses in the two columns. Circle the verb in the first column and underline the word that links the clauses in the second column.

a.	We know •	• i.	how well the party had gone.
b.	The man asked me •	• ii.	if Mum was missing us too.
c.	Everyone thought •	• iii.	what time it was.
d.	The police said •	• iv.	that the Earth goes round the sun.
e.	We wondered •	• v.	that they had found our car.

A subordinate clause that functions as a noun in a sentence is called a **noun clause**. It is usually the object of a saying or thinking verb.

 ISBN 978-93-5103-603-6

A noun clause is usually a statement, question or thought. Statements or thoughts often begin with the conjunction **that** and follow a verb such as **say**, **tell** or **think**. Spoken or unspoken questions begin with **if** or **whether** or with a question word such as **how** or **what**. They follow a verb such as **ask** or **wonder**.

Example Parul thought that the bearded man was my father.

We wondered how she managed to finish her work on time.

3. Underline the noun clause in each sentence.

   a. Raj said that it was snowing.
   b. She asked me if the train had left.
   c. Adam tells me that he wants to study astronomy.
   d. I wondered what was happening.
   e. They never told me they wanted my help.
   f. I guess you've all heard the news by now.
   g. Mr Shah enquired whether the flight was on time.
   h. I heard you'd been ill.
   i. You know perfectly well why I'm angry.
   j. Tell me where the keys are.

A noun clause can also be the subject of a verb.

Example What the child saw that night remained a mystery.

4. Underline the noun clause in each sentence.

   a. That he is a gifted writer is beyond doubt.
   b. What made her give up her job is something we shall never know.
   c. Where they spend their weekends is not our concern.
   d. How the boy saved the drowning child is an extraordinary story.
   e. That you practise hard is the most important thing.
   f. Why she was working so late is something we need to find out.
   g. How we're going to deal with the issue is the question.
   h. Where the neighbours are moving to doesn't concern us.
   i. That things may get worse is my greatest worry.
   j. How the hamster got out of its cage is a mystery.

Take Note

- To identify the noun clause in a sentence, we can ask the question **What?** after the verb e.g. Everybody knows (what?) **that he is a good guitarist.**
- The conjunction **that** is often omitted before a noun clause, e.g. He told Sultan **he would be working late tonight.**
- Verbs such as **know** and **tell** can be followed by a noun clause beginning with **if**, **whether** or a **wh**-question, e.g. I don't know **why she's so late.** Tell me **what's wrong.**

Take Note

Noun clauses act as nouns in various ways. A noun clause can be a complement after a **be** verb, e.g. The problem is **what shall we do next?** Noun clauses may sometimes be placed first in a sentence for emphasis, e.g. **How we're going to finish this project in time** I have no idea!

 ISBN 978-93-5103-603-6

Let's Practise

A. Underline the **noun clause** in each sentence.

1. I wonder how the animals survived the flood.
2. The teacher told Uma she must work harder.
3. Ronit asked if the swimming pool was open.
4. We were given the information that the fare had increased.
5. Why the *Titanic* sank is no longer a mystery.
6. I'm so pleased you two are getting married.
7. That Harish could be the thief had not occurred to me.
8. Mahesh wrote down what he had observed in his diary.

B. Complete each **noun clause** in the story with a set of words from the box below.

you meet him at the club	the tennis club is closed today
he wanted a game	I'll be able to let him know in time
would be the best alternative to tennis	you're making such a fuss
we meet there at four this afternoon	the arrangement is cancelled

"It's such a nuisance that ____________________," said Dilip. "I had already phoned Hasan to ask if ____________________, and he suggested that ____________________. Now I'll have to contact him and tell him ____________________. I don't think ____________________."

"I can't understand why ____________________," answered Usha.

"My suggestion is that ____________________. Then you can decide what ____________________."

Think & Share Play a "Did you Know?" game with your classmates. Each student has to say three things about themselves using noun clauses, in which only one is the truth. The others have to guess which one is a fact. For example, Did you know

- that I can play the guitar?
- that I can write the alphabet backwards in one minute?
- that I can speak eight languages fluently?

 ISBN 978-93-5103-603-6

9.6 Adjective clauses

Read the story.

Alice is the kind of girl **who loves pets.**

But the dog **that her aunt and uncle buy for her** looks big and frightening.

Charlie is a dog **that likes to be patted**, and he and Alice soon make friends.

Do you think Alice and Charlie have a good time together?

What kind of girl is Alice?

Which dog looks big and frightening?

What kind of dog is Charlie?

1. Note the highlighted clauses in the story above. Now underline the clause that describes a noun in each sentence.

   a. The house that Alice lives in is full of pets.

   b. People who keep pets should look after them properly.

   c. The dog that Uncle and Auntie bought looked frightening.

   d. Charlie was a dog that enjoyed a cuddle.

   e. Dogs like people who stroke them gently.

2. Underline the describing clause and circle the noun that it describes.

   Example (The lady) who lives next door has a cat.

   a. The bus which goes to the city centre is the S16.

   b. Miss Naik, who comes from Mumbai, is our new Maths teacher.

   c. I like teachers who explain things clearly.

   d. We once had a rabbit that lived in a hutch.

   e. Where is the book that I left on the table?

A subordinate clause that describes a noun in a sentence is called an **adjective clause**.

 ISBN 978-93-5103-603-6

An adjective clause says something about a person, place, animal or thing in the main clause of a sentence. Adjective clauses that refer to people usually begin with **who**, **whom** or **that**.

Example I need to speak to someone who knows all about computers.

3. Underline the adjective clause in each sentence.
   a. The police would like to interview anyone who witnessed the robbery.
   b. A dentist is a doctor who looks after people's teeth.
   c. The flight attendant, who is an old friend of mine, will help you find your baggage.
   d. Teachers really care about the children that they teach.
   e. Many children who took part in the competition won prizes.
   f. Shah Jahan, who belonged to the Mughal dynasty, built the Taj Mahal.
   g. The elderly man to whom we spoke just now is an experienced guide.
   h. You can never rely on a person who tells lies.
   i. The girl who won the race is our school's top athlete.
   j. Dan's sister, who lives in New York, just bought a new car.

Take Note
- Adjective clauses begin with the pronouns **that**, **who**, **whose**, **whom** or **which**. These are called **relative pronouns**.
- Adjective clauses are also known as **relative clauses**.

Adjective clauses that refer to animals or things usually begin with **which** or **that**.

Example The car which had an accident last night has been towed away.

4. Underline the adjective clause in each sentence.
   a. A hoe is a gardening tool that you use for digging up weeds.
   b. Where's the lamp which used to stand on the cabinet?
   c. Animals which hunt at night are called nocturnal animals.
   d. This is the house that Jack built.
   e. The new laptop that Sheena bought is already giving a lot of trouble.
   f. Let's meet at Krazy Café, which is just down the road.
   g. That house, which once belonged to a famous author, is now up for sale.
   h. Have you found the bag that you were looking for?

 ISBN 978-93-5103-603-6

Let's Practise

A. Underline the **adjective clause** in each sentence. Then circle the noun or pronoun it describes in the main clause.

1. The waitress who served us is called Indrani.
2. All students who can sing are invited to the audition.
3. The new mobile phone which he bought isn't working.
4. A spanner is a tool that is used for turning nuts and bolts.
5. What is the name of that girl who is sitting next to Aparna?
6. The train which got derailed yesterday was coming from Patna.

B. Complete each sentence with an **adjective clause** by adding **who** or **which** and a suitable group of words from the box below.

cooks food quickly	creates plays	performs gymnastic tricks
makes tiny objects look larger	studies animals	

1. An acrobat is a person ____________________.
2. A microwave is an oven ____________________.
3. A playwright is a writer ____________________.
4. A zoologist is a scientist ____________________.
5. A microscope is an instrument ____________________.

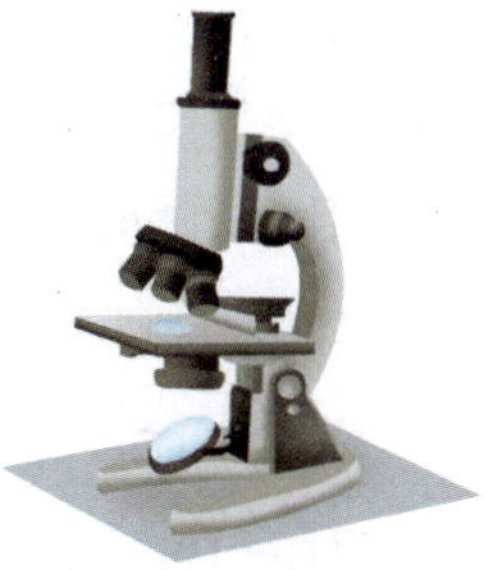

C. Rewrite each pair of sentences as one sentence using an adjective clause starting with **that** or **who**.

Example The book is lying on the table. It is about fish.

The book that is lying on the table is about fish.

1. The artist was painting a picture. He has finished it.
2. The doctor stitched my cut leg. He came from Sri Lanka.
3. A mystery friend phoned me. It turned out to be Rajiv.
4. We bought a washing machine. It was faulty.

 ISBN 978-93-5103-603-6

9.7 Adverb clauses

Read the story.

As the students of Newtown School arrived, they noticed the cracks in the walls.

When it rained the students and desks got wet, **because rain came in through the ceiling**.

Since the building was in such bad condition, the school moved to a new building.

Do you think the students missed their old school building?

When did the students notice the cracks on the walls?

Why did the students and desks get wet?

Why did the school move to a new building?

1. Note the highlighted clauses in the story above. Now underline the subordinate clause that says something about the action or situation in each sentence.

   a. The children noticed the cracks when they arrived in the morning.
   b. It was difficult to study while the ceiling was leaking.
   c. They moved into a new building because the old one was crumbling.
   d. The new building was much smarter than the old one was.
   e. The students were happier after they moved into the new building.

2. Match the clauses in the two columns. In the second column, circle the conjunction that links the clauses.

a. I'll collect your shopping	•	•	i. so that everyone gets to play.
b. Meena doesn't go near the pool	•	•	ii. in case I forget something.
c. Take turns on the computer	•	•	iii. that we couldn't sleep!
d. I always carry a shopping list	•	•	iv. because she can't swim.
e. We were so excited	•	•	v. if you give me the receipts.

A subordinate clause that says something about the action or situation in the main clause is called an **adverb clause**.

 ISBN 978-93-5103-603-6

An **adverb clause of time** answers the question "When?" It begins with a conjunction such as **after**, **as**, **as soon as**, **before**, **whenever**, **since**, **when** or **while**.

Take Note
An adverb clause can tell us about the time, place, reason or condition of an action. It can also help to make comparisons.

Example The children rushed out of their classrooms as soon as the bell rang.

3. Underline the adverb clause in each sentence.
   a. The roof leaks when it rains.
   b. We can discuss plans after you've had a meal.

An **adverb clause of place** answers the question "Where?" It begins with a conjunction such as **where**, **wherever**, **anywhere** or **everywhere**.

Example Go and stand where the other children are standing.

4. Underline the adverb clause in each sentence.
   a. The fairies live where the rainbow ends.
   b. The people followed him wherever he went.

An **adverb clause of reason** or **purpose** answers the question "Why?" or "What for?" It begins with a conjunction such as **because**, **as**, **since** or **so that**.

Example As it was a holiday, we went to see a play.

5. Underline the adverb clause in each sentence.
   a. I'm smiling because I'm happy.
   b. Nina went on the swing first, since she was the youngest.

An **adverb clause of condition** expresses a condition or possibility. It begins with a conjunction such as **if**, **as long as** or **unless**.

Example If you want to be a musician, you must practise regularly.

6. Underline the adverb clause in each sentence.
   a. You may stay here as long as you don't disturb me.
   b. I'll reach the restaurant by eight unless I have to work late.

An **adverb clause of comparison** forms part of a sentence comparing two actions, situations or events. It begins with the conjunction **than**.

Example The weather is hotter in Delhi than it is in Pune.

7. Underline the adverb clause in each sentence.
   a. My health is better than it used to be.
   b. A cheetah can run faster than a tiger can.

 ISBN 978-93-5103-603-6

Let's Practise

A. Underline the **adverb clause** in each sentence.

1. Whenever I see her, she reminds me of her mother.
2. Let's start the next chapter as we have some spare time.
3. She has grown her hair since I last saw her.
4. The plants will die if you don't water them.
5. Sadia works hard because she wants to do well.
6. When we reached the bus stop we saw Aisha.
7. As you've worked so hard you can have a rest.
8. Can cats see better in the dark than dogs can?

B. Complete each sentence with an **adverb clause** by adding a suitable group of words from the box below.

they wanted to	we can get a better view	the fighting is	you have the time
the band's flight has been delayed		the building had stood	

1. Soldiers must go where ______________________.
2. Do come and see me if ______________________.
3. In the past children could wander wherever ______________________.
4. The show is cancelled because ______________________.
5. Let's get a bit closer so that ______________________.
6. There was just a big hole where ______________________.

C. Complete the **adverb clauses** using your own words.

1. The job took longer than ______________________.
2. Stay where ______________________!
3. I'll call you if ______________________.
4. Since ______________________ you can tell us the story.
5. I decided to go for a jog because ______________________.

Think & Share Pair up with a classmate to play a matching game. Write down ten main clauses on a sheet of chart paper. Then write ten adverb clauses that match these main clauses on slips of paper and place them in a box. Take turns to pick up a slip from the box and match it to the correct main clause. The person who matches the most clauses correctly wins the game.

 ISBN 978-93-5103-603-6

9.8 Active and passive voice

Read the story.

Sally **had been dropped** off by the school bus. "Why **is** the ground **covered** with puddles?" she asked.

"The car **was being washed** by Dad," explained Mum.

"Now Dad is rushing because he **has been called** back to work," said Mum.

Why do you think Dad was called back to work?

What surprised Sally when she arrived home?

How did Mum explain the puddles?

Why was Dad rushing?

1. Note the highlighted verb forms in the story above. Now use them to complete the second sentence in each pair of sentences.

   a. Puddles cover the ground. The ground ______________ with puddles.

   b. The bus had dropped Sally off. Sally ______________ off by the bus.

   c. Dad was washing the car. The car ______________ by Dad.

2. Fill in the blanks using suitable verb forms from the box below.

were washed	was cleared	was taken

   a. Mum took Sheila to school.
      Sheila ______________ to school by Mum.

   b. The children cleared the snow.
      The snow ______________ by the children.

   c. Anil washed the sheets.
      The sheets ______________ by Anil.

When the **doer** of the action is the **subject** of the sentence, we say that the sentence is in the **active voice**. When we change the sentence round so that the **object** becomes the **subject**, and the action is done to the subject, we say the sentence is in the **passive voice**.

 ISBN 978-93-5103-603-6

Here is a set of tables that show how to change a sentence from the active into the passive voice. We use the **past participle** with one or more **helping verbs** to form the simple, continuous and perfect tenses.

Simple present

Active	Passive
I change. You/We/They change. He/She/It changes.	I am changed. You/We/They are changed. He/She/It is changed.

Present continuous

Active	Passive
I am changing. You/We/They are changing. He/She/It is changing.	I am being changed. You/We/They are being changed. He/She/It is being changed.

Present perfect

Active	Passive
I/You/We/They have changed. He/She/It has changed.	I/You/We/They have been changed. He/She/It has been changed.

Simple past

Active	Passive
I/He/She/It changed. You/We/They changed.	I/He/She/It was changed. You/We/They were changed.

Past continuous

Active	Passive
I/He/She/It was changing. You/We/They were changing.	I/He/She/It was being changed. You/We/They were being changed.

Past perfect

Active	Passive
I/You/He/She/It/We/They had changed.	I/You/He/She/It/We/They had been changed.

Simple future

Active	Passive
I/We shall change. You/He/She/It/They will change.	I/We shall be changed. You/He/She/It/They will be changed.

 ISBN 978-93-5103-603-6

Let's Practise

A. Read each sentence and underline the **verb** form. In the brackets, write **A** if it is active or **P** if it is passive.

1. The curry was being cooked by Mum. [ ]
2. The ringing of the telephone broke the silence. [ ]
3. The sun was hidden by the clouds. [ ]
4. The ambulance was taking the patient to hospital. [ ]
5. The streets are crowded with tourists in the summer. [ ]

B. Change the **active voice** into the **passive voice**. Use the preposition **by**.

Example Dad has painted the sitting room.

The sitting room has been painted by Dad.

1. The manager locks the shop every night.

____

2. Mum is driving the car.

____

3. Someone has altered the timetable.

____

4. Mrs Gupta checks all the pupils' names.

____

5. Mr Shah has written the report.

____

Take Note

- The **object** in the first sentence is the **subject** in the second sentence.
- The subject of the first sentence becomes, in the second sentence, the person or thing that the action is done **by**. The prepositions **with** and **in** are used too.

C. Change the **passive voice** into the **active voice**. If necessary, add words of your own to indicate the doer of the action.

1. I was hit on the head by a tennis ball.

____

2. The platforms are crowded with people during rush hour.

____

3. A picnic is being prepared by Komal.

____

4. The pages of the book had been torn by the baby.

____

5. The computer had been switched off by Rana.

____

Take Note

The doer of the action is often not mentioned in a sentence in the passive voice, e.g. The rubbish was removed (by someone).

 ISBN 978-93-5103-603-6

9.9 Simple and compound sentences

Read the story.

Jeff's car has broken down. He is checking the engine.

He can't see anything wrong and gives up.

Jeff phones a breakdown company and asks for help.

Remember!
A sentence can have one or more than one clause. Clauses that make complete sense by themselves are called coordinate clauses.

How soon do you think help will arrive?

Why is Jeff checking the engine?

Why does he look puzzled?

What does he do finally?

1. Note the sentences in the story above. Now underline the clauses in each sentence.
   a. Jeff's car broke down on a quiet country road.
   b. He lifted the bonnet and he looked at the engine.
   c. He couldn't identify the problem.
   d. He couldn't fix the engine himself, so he phoned a breakdown company.
   e. Help arrived and his car was fixed, so he drove happily on.

2. Circle the subjects and underline the main verbs. In the brackets, write how many clauses each sentence has.
   a. We got into the taxi and the driver took us to the airport. [ ]
   b. I found the end-of-term exams very difficult. [ ]
   c. On Saturdays I go shopping with Mum, or Dad takes me fishing. [ ]
   d. The colour scheme chosen by Jenna has an interesting effect. [ ]

Sentences that have only one clause are called **simple sentences**. Sentences that are made up of two or more coordinate clauses are called **compound sentences**.

 ISBN 978-93-5103-603-6

Let's Practise

A. Underline the **clause(s)** in each sentence. In the brackets, write **S** if the sentence is simple or **C** if it is compound.

1. Our flat was too small for us so we decided to move. [ ]
2. Neal and Nisha were going to go to the play but in the end they didn't. [ ]
3. According to the forecast it won't rain today but tomorrow it will. [ ]
4. In the beginning Kajal was very nervous about having swimming lessons. [ ]
5. It's a difficult problem and I can't promise success. [ ]
6. Use your imagination to solve this problem! [ ]
7. In my opinion taking exercise doesn't make you slimmer. [ ]
8. Either stay and help us or find some other occupation. [ ]

B. Combine each pair of **simple sentences** into a **compound sentence** using a suitable conjunction.

1. Anil asked Indira to go to a film with him. Indira was too busy.

   ____

2. Vipul's dog is sick. Vipul will have to take his dog to the vet.

   ____

3. Mum has made supper. Mum is setting the table.

   ____

4. Sunita lost an earring. Sunita found the earring later on the floor.

   ____

C. Break up each **compound sentence** into two **simple sentences** and write them on the blank below.

1. Can Uma come out to play or is she too tired?

   ____

2. Dad quite enjoys flying but finds the train more comfortable.

   ____

3. Mum's train is delayed so she will be late today.

   ____

4. I found a puppy and took it home.

   ____

Remember!

- Compound sentences are made up of coordinate clauses joined by the conjunctions **and**, **or**, **but** or **so**.
- If the subject of both clauses is the same person or thing, we often omit the subject from the second clause.

 ISBN 978-93-5103-603-6

9.10 Complex sentences

Read the story.

Julie is going for a cycle ride because she likes to keep fit.

She is puzzled when she comes to a signpost.

She meets a couple who have a map. The map shows her which track will take her back home.

What do you think Julie should do when she goes cycling the next time?

Why did she want to go for a cycle ride?

When was she puzzled?

What did the map show?

1. Read the sentences in the story above. Now underline the main clause and double-underline the subordinate clause in each sentence.

   a. Julie is going for a cycle ride because she likes to keep fit.

   b. She is puzzled when she comes to a signpost.

   c. She meets a couple who have a map.

   d. The map shows her which track will take her back home.

2. Match each main clause with a subordinate clause.

a. Whenever you go walking or cycling,	•	•	i. when you come to the junction.
b. I took the shirt back to the shop	•	•	ii. we can think about moving house.
c. We should punish people	•	•	iii. because it didn't fit.
d. Once Rumi has recovered,	•	•	iv. take a map with you.
e. Turn left	•	•	v. who drive recklessly.

A sentence that has a main clause and one or more subordinate clauses is called a **complex sentence**.

ISBN 978-93-5103-603-6

Let's Practise

A. Underline the **main clause** and double-underline the **subordinate clause(s)** in each complex sentence. In the brackets, write how many subordinate clauses it has.

1. You can't cross the river because the bridge is broken. [ ]
2. Everyone who applied will get a ticket. [ ]
3. When the tide is in, the beach is completely under water. [ ]
4. Although it was warm while the sun shone, it soon got cold. [ ]
5. Zainab told us that she had finished work on the book she was editing. [ ]

B. Make a **complex sentence** out of each pair of simple sentences. Use a suitable conjunction from the box below.

since	in case	so that	while

1. Why don't we go for a walk? The sun is shining.

____

2. You've shaved your beard off I last saw you.

____

3. Bring a spare pair of glasses. You lose one.

____

4. We'd better count the chairs. We know exactly how many there are.

____

C. Read each sentence. In the brackets, write **S** for simple, **CD** for compound or **CX** for complex.

1. The suggestion that he is a spy is ridiculous. [ ]
2. The children couldn't believe their eyes. [ ]
3. I got a fright when the telephone rang. [ ]
4. Shashi already speaks English well and is now learning German. [ ]
5. You have a lovely view from your balcony. [ ]
6. You should complain if the noise is so loud that you can't think. [ ]
7. The school is certainly better run than it used to be. [ ]
8. We work all day but we get paid so little in return. [ ]

 ISBN 978-93-5103-603-6

10 Questions

Let's Recall

- We can form questions with **question words** such as **what, who, whom, whose, which, why, how, when** or **where**. In questions, the verb usually comes before the subject.
- We can also form questions using different forms of the verbs **be**, **do** or **have**, either as helping verbs or as main verbs. These questions expect the answer **Yes** or **No**.
- Questions formed with the helping verbs **do/does/did** use the basic form of the main verb. Questions formed with the helping verbs **have/has/had** use the past participle of the main verb. Questions formed with the helping verbs **am/is/are/was/were** use the present participle of the main verb.

10.1 Revising questions

1. Fill in each blank with a suitable **question word**.
   a. ________ have you put my book?
   b. ________ did you spill on the floor?
   c. ________ has everybody stopped talking?
   d. ________ caused the accident?

Take Note
In most questions with helping verbs, the subject comes between the helping verb and the main verb. The exception to this order is a question where the question word is the subject of the verb, e.g. Who (subject) rang (verb) the bell?

2. Write the **question** that each sentence answers. Begin with a suitable **helping verb**.
   a. Gita has watered the flowers.
   ____
   b. The results were good.
   ____
   c. All dogs chase cats.
   ____

3. Fill in the blanks with **has**, **have** or **had** and the **past participle** form of the verb given in the brackets.
   a. ________ Mala and Rohit ________ their assignments before leaving on holiday yesterday? (finish)
   b. ________ she ________ her appointment letter yet? (receive)
   c. ________ you ________ your homework? (do)

 ISBN 978-93-5103-603-6

10.2 More about questions

Read the story.

"Look! Someone has dropped something!" cried Tom. "**Shall** we **see** what it is?"

"It's a wallet! **Should** we **try** to find the owner?" asked Tom. "Yes, we should," agreed Kate.

"Or **would** it **be** better to hand it over to the police?" Kate asked.

What would you have done with the wallet?

What did Tom ask when he saw something lying on the road?

What did he suggest they should do?

What did Kate ask?

1. Note the highlighted words in the story above. Now rewrite each sentence as a question, beginning with the underlined helping verb.

   a. That could be someone's wallet on the ground.

   ____

   b. We shall try to contact the owner.

   ____

   c. We should inform the police.

   ____

2. Underline the helping verb and double-underline the main verb in each question below.

   a. Can you see the sea from the top of the hill?
   b. May Deepak sleep at our house tonight?
   c. Could you turn the radio down a bit?
   d. Shall I tell you the shortest route to the museum?
   e. Will the timetable remain the same?

Questions formed with the helping verbs **shall, should, will, would, can, could** or **may** use the basic form of the main verb.

 ISBN 978-93-5103-603-6

Let's Practise

A. Rewrite each **question**, putting the words in the right order.

1. swimming today go we shall

____

2. baby hold I may the

____

3. books put we shelf the on back the should

____

4. change you bicycle can tyre a

____

5. this me bag carry for please you could

____

6. eclipse will sun tomorrow the there an be of

____

7. swing a like turn would the on you

____

8. discuss can we later this

____

Take Note
To confirm a statement, we sometimes add a short question after it. This is called a **question tag**. A positive statement has a negative question tag and a negative statement has a positive question tag, e.g. **It's** quite hot today, **isn't it**? She **isn't** leaving right away, **is she**?

B. Rewrite each sentence as a **negative question**. Use short forms where possible.

1. A new coat of paint would improve this room.

____

2. Sunil should help his mother more.

____

3. Your mum will be anxious about you.

____

4. Nandini could apply to the university for a grant.

____

5. This mobile phone can take photos.

____

Take Note
Negative questions beginning with a helping verb usually use short forms, e.g. Ca**n't** you ride a bike yet? Wo**n't** it be fun? Such questions usually expect the answer "Yes", but can also receive a negative answer.

Think & Share Pair up with a classmate to play the question game. Make flash cards with the helping verbs **shall**, **should**, **will**, **would**, **can**, **could** or **may** written on them and keep them face down on a table. Ask your partner to choose a noun and a verb. Then pick up a flash card and make a question with the helping verb written on it and the noun and verb chosen by your partner. Take turns to play this game.

 ISBN 978-93-5103-603-6

11 Punctuation

Let's Recall

- An **exclamation mark** (**!**) is used after greetings and expressions of strong feeling.
- An **apostrophe** (') is used with **-s** to show possession. We also use an apostrophe to join two words to make short forms. The apostrophe takes the place of the missing letter or letters.
- **Commas** (**,**) are used in lists of things. We also use commas before and after a group of words that describes a person or thing or when addressing somebody by their name. A comma also separates brief expressions, such as **yes**, **no**, **please** and **thank you**.

11.1 Revising punctuation

1. Rewrite each sentence using the correct **punctuation** and **capital letters**.

   a. you will need a piece of fabric a needle thread and a pair of scissors

   ____

   b. now write down my address

   ____

   c. how you have grown Sita

   ____

   d. thank you Miss Khan for that information

   ____

   e. our new series Alpha Grammar has a different approach

   ____

   f. quiet please

   ____

   g. what a mess that cat Freda has made of the carpet

   ____

   h. Romila who has curly hair lives on the floor above

   ____

   i. is this your bag Harish

   ____

 ISBN 978-93-5103-603-6

2. Rewrite each sentence using an **apostrophe** where needed.

a. Were preparing for the childrens party.

____

b. Well be meeting at Juhis house.

____

c. The juniors are happy now that theyre allowed to play seniors games.

____

d. Dad couldnt mend Haris kite.

____

e. Youre welcome to use my sons bicycle.

____

f. I shouldnt have forgotten Saras birthday.

____

g. I didnt watch the mens singles final.

____

3. Rewrite each sentence expanding the **short form** into its full form.

Example Sheela's cancelled the meeting.

Sheela has cancelled the meeting.

a. The cat miaows when it's time for its tea and purrs when it's had its tea.

____

b. Here's the money that Uncle Joe's sent you.

____

c. I heard you'd won a prize.

____

d. There's been no rain for a week.

____

e. Mum's going to find out the details.

____

f. She'd better stay in bed if she's unwell.

____

g. I'd like to be able to fly.

____

Take Note

The form **'s** can be short for **is** or **has**. E.g. **He's going** means "He is going" and **He's gone** means "He has gone". Similarly, **it's** can mean "it is" or "it has", whereas **its** is a possessive adjective (e.g. This bottle has lost **its** top). The form **'d** can be short for **had** or **would**. E.g. **She'd gone** means "She had gone" and **She'd go** means "She would go".

 ISBN 978-93-5103-603-6

11.2 Quotation marks

Read the story.

The newsreader said, "A young man was injured in Mumbai today by a lorry on the Western Express Highway."

She went on, "Witnesses say the driver was breaking the speed limit."

She added, "The police have asked anyone with information about the accident to dial 100."

Why do you think the police are asking for information from people who saw the accident?

What words did the newsreader use when she started reading the news?
What information did she give about the driver of the lorry?
What did she say about the police?

1. Note the words in green in the pictures above. Now underline the actual words of the speaker in each of the following sentences.
   a. There was an accident on the Western Express Highway today, said the announcer.
   b. She read on, A young man was injured.
   c. The lorry-driver was speeding, she added.
   d. The police have asked anyone who saw the accident to dial 100, she said.

2. Note the highlighted punctuation marks in the sentences in the pictures above. Rewrite each of the following sentences using these punctuation marks.
   a. What time is it? asked Dilip.

      ____

   b. Thank goodness the exams are over! said Gita.

      ____

   c. I'm going shopping today, announced Shanti.

      ____

When we state the exact words someone uses, we put the punctuation marks (" ") at the beginning and end of them. These punctuation marks are called **quotation marks**.

 ISBN 978-93-5103-603-6

Let's Practise

A. Underline the words of the speakers in the story. Then add the missing **quotation marks**.

Hello! I'm home! called Mohit. Where are you?

I'm in the study, called Hema. Have you had a good day?

Not bad, he replied, coming into the study.

Well, I'm exhausted, said Hema. How about a cup of tea?

Lovely, answered Mohit. Let me help you.

Thanks, said Hema. Do you have to go out again this evening? she asked.

No. Let's spend the evening in front of the television, said Mohit.

B. Rewrite each sentence adding the missing **quotation marks**.

1. Have you eaten anything unusual recently? asked Dr Reddy.

   ____

2. Komal said to Kiran, It's your turn to make dinner tonight.

   ____

3. Please don't tell anybody, she begged.

   ____

4. Peter said, It's too early to get up.

   ____

5. You could move house, suggested Tim.

   ____

6. Who can tell me when the holidays start? asked Mum.

   ____

7. I can't believe you missed your flight! exclaimed Tom.

   ____

8. Here you are! said Harry. We've been looking for you.

   ____

Take Note

- If the spoken words come before the speaker and verb, we put a comma/ question mark/ exclamation mark after the spoken words, before the closing quotation mark. E.g. "It is raining," said Ravi.
- If the spoken words come after the speaker and verb, we put a comma after the speaker, before the opening quotation mark. E.g. Ravi said, "It is raining."
- Quotation marks are also known as **inverted commas**, **speech marks** or **quote marks**.

Think & Share Pair up with a classmate to write a short dialogue between two people. Make sure you use quotation marks and other punctuation marks as needed. Then act out the dialogue in front of the class.

 ISBN 978-93-5103-603-6

Review 3

1. Circle the correct **preposition** to complete each sentence.
   a. The path runs (against / along) the riverside for several kilometres.
   b. Nikhil held (onto / upon) the rope with all his might.
   c. The speed restriction remains in place (onto / until) 6.30 p.m.
   d. Our team is playing (opposite / against) the Hasimpur team next week.
   e. There (upon / over) the table lay the important envelope.
   f. The soup is done. Take the pan (along / off) the stove.
   g. The Chinese restaurant (onto / round) the corner is my favourite.
   h. They sat (against / opposite) each other on the bus and chatted all the way to school.
   i. Their living room is larger (than / off) ours.

2. Fill in each blank with a suitable **complex preposition** from the box below.

on top of	along with	up to	next to	out of	in front of

   a. Here's a photo of me standing ____________ the Taj Mahal.
   b. The Railway Hotel was built ____________ the station.
   c. We all got ____________ the car to see what was happening.
   d. Asha hid the present ____________ a cupboard.
   e. A stranger came ____________ me and asked me the time.
   f. I'm going to the gym. Would you like to come ____________ me?

3. Underline the **conjunctions** in each sentence.
   a. We can either turn left or continue straight on.
   b. Ridhi likes both singing and dancing.
   c. Neither Alan nor Rohit turned up for the party.
   d. We not only visited Grandmother today, but also went to the park.
   e. You may have either an apple or a light snack before dinner.
   f. Farah reads both classical and modern literature.

 ISBN 978-93-5103-603-6

4. Complete each sentence using a **conjunction** from the top box and a **clause** from the lower box.

before	and	because	when

they left for Dubai	she drives them to school
the sun rises	you have behaved so well

a. The sky lights up ______________________________.

b. I will take you to the park ______________________________.

c. They had dinner ______________________________.

d. Mahima dresses her two daughters ______________________________.

5. In these sentences, underline the **main clause** or the **coordinate clauses**, and double-underline the **subordinate clause**.

a. As soon as I set out for my walk, it began to rain.

b. Neeraj loves animals and wants to become a vet.

c. I don't believe that Zara intended any harm.

d. You may phone Grandmother when you get home tonight, but please be polite.

e. People who live in glass houses shouldn't throw stones.

f. I've set aside the books I want to keep.

g. I can't explain now because it's too complicated.

h. As it's Saturday, you may stay up late.

i. The lady wanted to know if the park was open to the public.

j. Would you like a meal now or would you prefer to eat later?

6. Underline the **subordinate clause** in each sentence. In the brackets, write **N** if it is a noun clause, **Adj** if it is an adjective clause or **Adv** if it is an adverb clause.

a. I want you to know that I'm always ready to help you. [ ]

b. Phone me as soon as you get home. [ ]

c. The policeman I spoke to gave me directions to the museum. [ ]

d. Turn right when you reach the crossroads, then take the first left. [ ]

e. Tell me everything you know about it. [ ]

f. I don't understand what you mean. [ ]

g. The hand that rocks the cradle rules the world. [ ]

h. As the tide went out, the seashells were left strewn on the beach. [ ]

 ISBN 978-93-5103-603-6

7. Change each **active** sentence into a **passive** sentence, using **by** to add the doer of the action.

a. Grandfather was trimming the hedge.

____

b. Everyone heard the terrible scream.

____

c. The association will inform residents about the changes.

____

d. A passer-by filmed the incident on his phone.

____

8. Change each **passive** sentence into an **active** sentence.

a. The chariot is being drawn by two horses.

____

b. The prizes will be given out by the chief guest.

____

c. The roads are being repaired by the municipal council.

____

d. The Chatterjis will be received by Mum and Dad in Delhi.

____

9. Combine each pair of simple sentences into a **compound sentence** using a suitable **conjunction**.

a. Dad went out to buy some medicines. The pharmacy was shut.

____

b. Would you like a meal now? Would you like to unpack first?

____

c. I unwrapped the gift. I opened the box.

____

10. Combine each pair of simple sentences into a **complex sentence** using a suitable **conjunction**.

a. We helped the victims of the earthquake. We felt it our duty.

____

b. Let's get the application forms. The office is open.

____

c. You've lost your pen. I've bought you a new one.

____

 ISBN 978-93-5103-603-6

11. Rewrite each **question**, putting the words in the right order.

a. that making you stop dreadful noise will

____

b. we hear the tomorrow shall results

____

c. the baggage you could help me get into car the

____

d. lunch we meet can one for week next day

____

12. Rewrite each sentence as a **negative question** with a short form.

a. Durga likes hot curries.

____

b. Sarthak was at the meeting.

____

c. The baby will stop crying.

____

d. Meena can swim in deep water.

____

13. Add the missing **quotation marks** in the story.

I've got some exciting news! shouted Sia, bursting into the room.

Sarah looked up from her book. What is it? she asked.

Sia settled down on the sofa and said excitedly, Dad's taking Mum and me to Tokyo in the holidays.

Lucky you! sighed Sarah. What will you do there?

Sia fished out a holiday brochure from her pocket and said, Lots of things. I'm going to see everything that's mentioned in this brochure.

Spot the Error

14. There is a mistake in each sentence. Underline it and rewrite the passage correctly in your notebook.

"Mum, could you please come here? said Gita. "I'll come unless I've fed the baby," replied Mum. Gita was tryng to do her English homework. She preferred to study Physics along with English, but she had an English test the next day. Written essays was not something she enjoyed. Wouldn't it be better if she had a different topic. Either Mum would have to help her nor she would have to ask Dad.

 ISBN 978-93-5103-603-6

12 Comprehension

12.1 Finding information and concluding

- When you are asked about a certain thing in the text, you read it again and find the correct details. This is called finding information.
- As you read a text, you should think carefully about the facts and details and decide what they actually mean. This is called concluding.

Read the formal letter.

Central Water Board
35 MG Road
Dehradun
21 August 2016

Mr Harsh Sharma
37 South Avenue
Dehradun

Dear Mr Sharma,

Subject: Interruption of water supply to Block 2, Mountain Heights

This is to inform you that new water pipes are to be laid to your block of flats, replacing the old worn pipes that connect with the mains water pipes under the street.

The work is scheduled to take place on Wednesday 14 September 2016 between 9.00 a.m. and 6.00 p.m. Your water supply will be cut off for that period of time.

If this is likely to cause severe difficulties, please contact us at 0135-2481-5480. We shall make arrangements for a tanker to supply water to you. For any other queries, please contact our supervisor at 0135-2481-5482.

Yours faithfully,
K A Ramakrishnan
Secretary
Central Water Board

Take Note

A formal letter

- uses formal, polite and straightforward language.
- is usually divided into paragraphs.
- has the date on which the letter is written.
- has the sender's and the receiver's name and address
- also has the full name and official title of the sender.

 ISBN 978-93-5103-603-6

Answer the questions.

1. What is the information being conveyed in the letter?

____

2. When is the work scheduled to take place in Block 2?

____

3. Why are the water pipes being replaced? Tick the correct answer.

   a. The water pipes currently in use are old and worn.

   b. The new water pipes are more efficient and long-lasting.

   c. The water from the current pipes is not enough for the entire block of flats.

4. You can conclude that the Central Water Board is replacing the pipes in a systematic manner because _______________

____

5. How can you conclude that the Central Water Board is concerned about the welfare of the residents?

____

6. How can you conclude that the work will impact daytime activities on Wednesday 14 September?

____

7. What is the meaning of **severe**? Tick the correct answer.

   a. serious b. little c. slight

8. From the letter, find and write the following:

   a. a simple sentence

   ____

   b. a complex sentence

   ____

9. Find four noun phrases in the letter.

   a. _______________ c. _______________

   b. _______________ d. _______________

Think!
In order to find information, you
- underline the keywords in the question. They will tell you what information you need to find.
- find those keywords in the text.
- carefully read the information given in the sentence and decide on the answer.

Think!
In order to conclude, you
- understand what you are making a conclusion about.
- find the facts and details from the text.
- decide what exactly the facts and details mean.

 ISBN 978-93-5103-603-6

12.2 Predicting and summarising

- As you read a story, it is important to understand what is happening in it and try to think what might happen next. This is called predicting.
- When you talk about what you have read, you need to put together the main points in as few words as possible. This is called summarising.

Read the narrative.

Take Note
A narrative
- is an account of a real or imaginary event.
- tells the story in the order in which things happened.
- often ends with a problem being solved.

Finding Aunt Uma

One day Mum looked at the clock and said, "Oh dear, I didn't realise that it was already 10.30! I have a dental appointment in fifteen minutes' time, and I should have taken this dress material round to Aunt Uma in Rajouri Road. Ayesha, could you take it to Aunt Uma instead? She needs it urgently. She wants to make a dress for your cousin's birthday this weekend."

Eleven-year-old Ayesha was busy with her homework, but she said, "Okay, Mum." So Mum set off for the dentist's and Ayesha set off for Aunt Uma's, carrying the dress material. Aunt Uma had recently moved to Rajouri Road, and Ayesha had not been to her house. However, she knew it was No. 21. It was ten minutes' walk away, and it was on a hill. At last she reached No. 20.

"Aunt Uma is just next door," she thought. She rang the bell of the next house. It was a long time before the door was answered. Then she got a fright. The door was opened by a tall, fierce-looking man who was a complete stranger.

"Where's Aunt Uma?" asked Ayesha. "I mean … er … Mrs Shankar?"

"I don't know any Mrs Shankar," said the man impatiently. "She certainly doesn't live here!" Then he said, a bit more kindly, "What number are you looking for?"

"No. 21," said Ayesha nervously. The man actually smiled.

"This is No. 22!" he said. "No. 21 is across the road."

 ISBN 978-93-5103-603-6

"Of course!" thought Ayesha. "The odd numbers are on the other side!" She thanked the man, crossed the street and found No. 21 straightaway. She rang the bell, and there was Aunt Uma in the doorway. She was glad to see Ayesha, and delighted with the dress material. She gave Ayesha a glass of cold juice before letting her walk back home.

Answer the questions.

1. Which of these things do you think Mum would have done if Ayesha had not been able to deliver the dress material? Tick the correct answer.
   a. She would have taken the material to Aunt Uma herself that very day.
   b. She would have asked Ayesha to go and find the right house again.
   c. She would have made the dress herself.
   d. She would have asked Aunt Uma to come over and collect the material.

Think!
In order to predict, you
- find information related to the question.
- think about the information and ask yourself, "What is the writer suggesting might happen?"

2. Do you think the tall, fierce-looking man would have helped Ayesha find Aunt Uma's house? Support your answer with a detail from the story.

____

____

3. Do you think Aunt Uma was able to make the dress in time for Ayesha's cousin's birthday? Give one reason for your answer.

____

____

4. Which fact would you NOT include in a summary of the second paragraph?
   a. Eleven-year-old Ayesha was busy with her homework.
   b. Aunt Uma's house was ten minutes' walk away.
   c. Aunt Uma had recently moved to Rajouri Road.
   d. Ayesha knew the house number was No. 21.

5. Which phrase do you think best summarises the nature of the man Ayesha spoke to?
   a. friendly and kind
   b. hot-tempered and violent
   c. irritable but caring
   d. friendly but suspicious

Think!
In order to summarise, you
- look carefully at the information in the text.
- decide on what is important and how it is connected.
- leave out any unnecessary information.

 ISBN 978-93-5103-603-6

6. Write a summary of how Ayesha managed to find Aunt Uma.

____

____

____

____

____

____

____

____

7. What is the opposite of an **odd number**?

____

8. What does **fierce-looking** mean? Tick the correct answer.

a. afraid b. fearful c. frightening-looking

9. From the narrative, find and write the following:

a. a noun clause

____

b. an adjective clause

____

10. Find a sentence that consists of three coordinate clauses in the last paragraph and write it down.

____

____

11. Read each sentence. In the brackets, write **P** if it is in the passive voice and **A** if it is in the active voice. Then rewrite the sentence, changing its voice.

a. Ayesha rang the bell. [ ]

____

b. After a long wait, the door was answered. [ ]

____

c. The door was opened by a tall, fierce-looking man. [ ]

____

d. Aunt Uma gave Ayesha a glass of cold juice. [ ]

____

 ISBN 978-93-5103-603-6

12.3 Identifying cause and effect and distinguishing between fact and opinion

- If you want to understand what you read, you must be able to identify how one thing (the cause) makes another thing (the effect) happen in a series of events. This is called identifying cause and effect.
- When you read, you should try to understand the difference between what is true and what someone believes is true. This is called distinguishing between fact and opinion.

Read the playscript.

Take Note

A playscript

- uses dialogue. The words are said by two or more people. In everyday life, this is called a conversation.
- is written to be performed in front of an audience.

Coffee and Conversation

(Scene: A railway compartment. Vijay, a college student, is sitting alone reading. The train has stopped at a station. Durga, a girl of about the same age, opens the door and gets in.)

Vijay: Let me help you with your luggage. Shall I put your suitcase on the luggage rack?

Durga: Thanks so much. Is this seat taken?

Vijay: No, do sit down. (Durga sits down opposite Vijay.) Oh, look! You've dropped your book! (He picks it up.) Ah, *Just So Stories*, by Rudyard Kipling. Do you like Kipling's books?

Durga: Oh yes, Kipling's *Jungle Book* is one of my favourite books.

Vijay: That's good to hear. People hardly read books nowadays. We are constantly surfing the Internet and typing away on the phone or on the computer.

Durga: Well, I must confess that I'm quite a fan of computers myself. I only carry books to read when I'm travelling.

 ISBN 978-93-5103-603-6

Vijay: Of course, computers are a boon, and books are available on the Internet, but there's nothing quite like reading a printed book.

Durga: I don't agree. A lot of paper is used to print books and magazines, for which thousands of trees are cut down. Reading books on computers, mobile phones and tablets saves the environment.

Vijay: Yes, you're right there. But staring at a screen for hours damages the eyes. And spending hours on the Internet is certainly not good for your health.

Durga: True. I guess it's important to strike a balance. Are you at the university?

Vijay: Yes, I'm in my second year, I'm studying Chemistry. Why don't we get together for a coffee when term starts again?

Durga: That would be great. Let's exchange e-mail addresses.

Answer the questions.

1. Why are people reading fewer books nowadays? Tick the correct cause.
   a. Not enough books are being published nowadays.
   b. Authors have stopped writing books.
   c. People prefer watching films to reading books.
   d. People prefer surfing the Internet on their computers and mobile phones.

2. According to Durga, what is the effect of book printing on the environment?

   ____

   ____

3. List two effects of spending too much time on computers, according to Vijay.
   a. ____________________
   b. ____________________

4. Which sentence states a fact? Tick the correct answer.
   a. *Just So Stories* is a book by Rudyard Kipling.
   b. Computers are a boon.
   c. Nothing can replace the pleasure of reading a book.

5. Which sentence states an opinion? Tick the correct answer.
   a. *The Jungle Book* is written by Rudyard Kipling.
   b. A lot of paper is used to print books and magazines.
   c. Reading books on computers, mobile phones and tablets saves the environment.

Think!
In order to identify cause and effect, you
- must understand how one thing leads to another and how they are connected in the text.
- look for keywords in the question and underline them.
- find words in the text that are connected to these keywords.

Think!
In order to distinguish between fact and opinion, you
- check if the statement can be proved to be true. If it can be proved, it is a fact.
- check if the statement expresses what someone thinks or believes. If it cannot be proved to be true, it is an opinion.

 ISBN 978-93-5103-603-6

6. Is the statement "We are constantly surfing the Internet and typing away on the phone or on the computer." a fact or an opinion? Explain your answer.

____

____

7. Read each statement. In the brackets, write **F** if it expresses a fact or **O** if it expresses an opinion.

   a. Kipling's *The Jungle Book* is one of my favourite books. [ ]
   b. I'm studying Chemistry. [ ]
   c. I guess it's important to strike a balance. [ ]
   d. People hardly read books nowadays. [ ]
   e. I'm in my second year. [ ]
   f. Books are available on the Internet. [ ]

8. Find one question from the text that asks for a fact.

____

9. Find one question from the text that asks for an opinion.

____

10. What does the word **boon** mean? Tick the correct answer.

    a. blessing   b. help   c. annoyance

11. Find a word from the text that means:

    a. all the time ______________________________
    b. hurts ______________________________

12. Rewrite each pair of sentences as one sentence, using one of the pairs of conjunctions from the box.

not only...but also	either...or	both...and

    a. Vijay studies at the university. Durga studies at the university.

    ____

    b. Spending hours on the Internet is harmful for the eyes. Spending hours on the Internet is not good for your health.

    ____

    c. People spend all their time on their phones. People spend all their time on their computers.

    ____

 ISBN 978-93-5103-603-6

12.4 Identifying the main idea and understanding the writer's point of view and purpose

- There are many ideas in a text, but you should try to find the one idea that links them. This is called identifying the main idea.
- When you read, you should try to think like the writer to work out how and what they feel and believe about the subject and why they wrote the text. This is called understanding the writer's point of view and purpose.

Read the notice.

PREVENT ANIMAL CRUELTY!

Are you willing to support us in setting up **a shelter for stray animals** and **animals that are cruelly treated**?

Thousands of animals in our city are suffering. Dogs are beaten to death. Donkeys are crippled by carrying burdens that are far too heavy for them. Abandoned dogs and cats wander through our streets with nowhere to go. Some starve, and many die, or are badly hurt in traffic accidents.

We are planning an **animal shelter on the outskirts of the city**, where these animals can be taken and looked after, so that they can regain their health.

We are looking for:

- **Volunteers** to identify animals at risk
- **Helpers** to look after animals at the shelter
- **Donations** – whatever you can spare – to pay for the shelter.

Come and hear all about it at a **public meeting** at the **Central Hall, Lansdowne Road,** on **Saturday 15 October 2016** at **2 p.m.**

Phone 90123 01234 if you want to offer help or donations.
THE ANIMAL WELFARE SOCIETY, 2 KUMAR STREET RAMPUR

Take Note

A notice
- has an eye-catching heading.
- gives brief but complete information.
- uses language that is to the point.
- gives the name and details of the authority that is issuing the notice.

 ISBN 978-93-5103-603-6

Answer the questions.

1. What is the main idea of the notice?
   a. Stray animals in the city are suffering.
   b. We need to prevent cruelty to animals.
   c. Every city should have an animal shelter.
   d. Stray animals should be put in an animal shelter.

2. What is the main idea of the second paragraph of the notice?

   ____

   ____

3. Why do you think an animal shelter is needed?

   ____

   ____

4. What do you think is the writer's point of view about animals?

   ____

   ____

5. What do you think is the main purpose behind inviting people to attend the meeting at the Central Hall?

   ____

   ____

6. What kind of person do you think the writer is? Give one reason for your answer.

   ____

   ____

   ____

   ____

   ____

7. What does the word **abandoned** mean? Tick the correct answer.
   a. neglected b. rejected by their owners c. banned

8. Underline the adjective clauses in the following sentences.
   a. The animal shelter will take care of animals that are suffering.
   b. The writer is looking for volunteers who can identify animals at risk.
   c. People who care about animals should come to the public meeting.

Think!
In order to identify the main idea, you
- read the text. Then ask yourself, "What is it mainly about?"
- look at the title. A good title often tells you what the text is about.

Think!
In order to understand the writer's point of view and purpose, you
- try to think like they do.
- underline the details and information that are related to the question and draw a conclusion regarding what the writer thinks or believes.

 ISBN 978-93-5103-603-6

13 Composition

13.1 E-mail

An e-mail is a letter sent from one computer-user to another via an electronic network. The word e-mail is a short form of "electronic mail". E-mails should be brief, clear and error-free.

Take Note
A typical e-mail has four main parts:
1. Subject line
2. Greeting and introductory paragraph
3. Body
4. Ending

From: Zeinab <zeinabkhatun@mint.com>
To: Shashi <shashikala@abc.com>
Subject: Picture on request
Date: 2 Nov 2016 at 10:00

Subject line
Make sure your subject line refers to the message.

Hi Shashi,

Thanks for your message of 31 October, and I apologise for taking so long to reply.

Greeting and introductory paragraph
Greet the person. If you are replying to an e-mail, thank them for their last message.

The problem was that I couldn't immediately get hold of the picture you wanted to see, because my tutor had it and she was away on holiday. I've now scanned it, and am attaching it. I hope you can open the attachment. Do let me know if I can help in any other way.

Body
Introduce the main topic and deal with it. Add anything else that is relevant.

I look forward to seeing you on Saturday at Kavita's party.

Best wishes,
Zeinab

Ending
Mention any future arrangements with the person, and sign off with a suitable good-bye greeting.

 ISBN 978-93-5103-603-6

Let's Practise

Use the outline to write an e-mail thanking a friend for a birthday present they have sent you.

Subject line: mention what the e-mail is about

Greeting and introductory paragraph: greet your friend – thank them for the birthday present

Body: mention what the birthday present is – say why you like it – describe briefly how you spent your birthday

Ending: make plans to meet your friend – add a good-bye greeting and sign off

 ISBN 978-93-5103-603-6

13.2 Essay

An essay is a piece of writing based on a particular topic. An essay can be an explanation of an idea or an analysis of something. It can be written to persuade the reader to accept the writer's point of view or to present an argument regarding a specific issue.

Take Note
An essay has three main parts:
1. Introduction
2. Body
3. Conclusion

TV Serials

Do you enjoy TV serials? Or do you think they are silly? Let us have a look at the good and bad aspects of TV serials.

Introduction
Start with a lively first paragraph that makes the reader want to find out more.

The special thing about TV serials is that, although they are imaginary, their stories keep going as though the characters were really living their daily lives. This is what grips viewers. When they watch one episode, they feel they must know what happens next. They must discover how Devesh copes with his mother's death. They can't wait to hear if Madhu's baby has arrived safely. They want to hear that Rahul gets punished for telling lies about his brother.

In order to keep their audience interested, the writers of these serials fill the storyline with lots of sensational events. They also end the episodes in the middle of the most dramatic moment so that the next episode becomes a must-watch. Fans even become addicted, and there may be tensions within families when other members want to watch a different channel at the same time.

Body
Think of sensible and interesting points that contribute to different sides of the discussion.

One good thing is that the storyline sometimes deals with genuine social issues that can raise awareness and allow open discussion. However, we should always remember that, real as they seem, these dramas are not real life.

Conclusion
Come to a conclusion that reflects what you have said and sums things up.

 ISBN 978-93-5103-603-6

Let's Practise

Use the outline to write an essay.

My Favourite TV Programme

Introduction: mention the name of the programme – give details about it – mention what it is about

Body: explain why you like the programme – support your argument by describing one episode – strengthen your point by comparing it with other programmes

Conclusion: discuss the larger benefits of watching the programme – mention the popular rating of the programme – draw a conclusion about the future of the programme

 ISBN 978-93-5103-603-6

13.3 Story

A story is an account of a real or imaginary event or series of events.

Take Note

A typical story has three main parts:

1. Beginning
2. Middle
3. Ending

The Cross-country Race

It was a special day at school, the day of the annual cross-country race. It meant seven kilometres of running through the countryside and back to school. Javed had been practising hard for weeks. Everyone believed he had a chance of winning, but he was not actually the favourite.

Sanjay had always been a good athlete, and was the school champion in athletics. He and Javed usually trained together, and competed against each other in a friendly way. Javed hoped to win the trophy this year and surprise his family.

Beginning Make the beginning of the story interesting. Set the scene and explain the background to the event.

The schoolchildren gathered excitedly around the starting line as the participants lined up for the race. The gym master gave the signal to start, and thirty boys ran down the driveway and out of the gates. Javed and Sanjay soon left the others behind them. On they ran, but Sanjay was always ahead of Javed. Then, on their way down a hill, Javed saw Sanjay trip and fall. His first idea was to pass Sanjay and win the race. However, Sanjay had injured his ankle and could hardly walk. Javed could not leave him there. So he put his arm round Sanjay, and together they finished the course, Javed walking and Sanjay hobbling beside him. The other runners caught up with them and passed them easily.

Middle Develop the events in the story.

So they were last instead of first, but it didn't matter, and everybody praised Javed for being so unselfish.

Ending Show a clear resolution.

 ISBN 978-93-5103-603-6

Let's Practise

Use the outline to write a story.

Resisting Temptation

Beginning: it is exam time – Mrs Gupta, the head teacher, has asked to see Priya in her room about something

Middle: Mrs Gupta's door is open but she is not there – Priya waits in the room – she sees the English exam paper on Mrs Gupta's desk

Ending: Priya is tempted to look at the questions – she stops herself from doing so – Mrs Gupta comes back to her room – she talks to her about an inter-school debating competition – Priya comes out of the room – she feels relieved

 ISBN 978-93-5103-603-6

13.4 Autobiography

An autobiography is the story of someone's life written by that person. You can also imagine yourself to be an animal or object and write their autobiography.

Take Note
A typical autobiography has three main parts:
1. Beginning
2. Middle
3. Ending

The Autobiography of a Puppy

The first thing I clearly remember as a young puppy is Bobo, a little teddy bear that I used to play with in my cage in a pet shop. Whenever anyone stepped into the shop, I made sure to be on my best behaviour because I wanted a new family. I was there for weeks and many people petted me, but no one took me home. I had started to lose hope when a little girl entered with her mother. I got up and wagged my tail. The girl laughed and rubbed my belly. Oh, that felt so good! She seemed kind and I really wanted to go home with her, but after looking at all the pets, they went away.

Beginning
Introduce yourself, using the first person. Talk about your background and early life.

The little girl visited me every day after school. She liked to play with Bobo and me. Many other people visited the pet shop and some of them played with me, but I liked the little girl the best. She told me that she had been working very hard at school and doing her household tasks on time to prove to her parents that she was responsible enough to take care of me.

One day, a woman walked in and smiled at me. I recognised her as the girl's mother! She went up to the man behind the desk and pointed at me. Next thing I knew, the man had opened the cage and handed me to her. I licked her face and she was delighted!

Middle
Describe the major events in your life so far in sequence. Give interesting details. Think from the point of view of the speaker.

I was so excited! I was finally getting a new family! She took me home with her and called the little girl. "Happy birthday, Radha! You've been a very good and hardworking girl, so here is a present from your father and me," she said as she handed me to the girl. Radha thanked her mother and hugged me. That day, she and I both got a wonderful gift – a best friend!

Ending
Provide a strong ending. It may be satisfying or surprising.

 ISBN 978-93-5103-603-6

Let's Practise

Use the outline to write the autobiography of a book.

The Autobiography of a Book

Beginning: introduce yourself – mention the title on your cover and the name of your author – mention what your content is about – describe how you were made and where you were sent

Middle: describe your time on a shelf in a bookshop – give details about the person who bought you – say how you felt about the way you were treated – talk about the people who handled you

Ending: describe your present condition – share your thoughts and feelings about your life and experiences

 ISBN 978-93-5103-603-6

13.5 Application

An application is a formal letter asking to be considered for a job that has been advertised.

Take Note
An application has three parts:
1. Greeting and introductory paragraph
2. Body
3. Ending and signing off

BKG Towers
GK Marg
Srinagar
6 March 2016

Farhan Khan
Secretary to the Director
The Museum of Ethnology

Dear Sir,

Subject: Application for a voluntary job

I am writing with reference to your advertisement last week in the *Schools Gazette* for volunteers to help with the reorganisation of the museum's displays, during the school holidays.

Greeting and introductory paragraph
Formally address the person acting as the contact. Explain where you saw their advertisement.

I would like to apply for one of these voluntary jobs. I am interested in both design and archaeology, and would value the opportunity to develop my ability and knowledge in these fields. My Art teacher Mrs Vadera and my History teacher Mr Shah have both agreed to write a recommendation, if you need one.

Body
Say you would like to apply and why, and give the name of anyone who has agreed to recommend you.

I would be very happy to be included in your team of voluntary helpers. I look forward to hearing from you.

Yours sincerely,
Harleen Singh

Ending and signing off
Say how you would appreciate the job, and sign off formally.

 ISBN 978-93-5103-603-6

Let's Practise

Use the outline to write an application for a job as a voluntary helper at a children's nursery.

Greeting and introductory paragraph: give your address and details – mention the date and the subject – give the details of the person you are addressing – greet the person formally and mention where you saw the vacancy

Body: explain your reason for applying – mention a recommendation, if any

Ending and signing off: thank the person for their time – round off your letter with a word of appreciation

 ISBN 978-93-5103-603-6

Review 4

1. Read the formal letter and answer the questions below in your notebook.

Srinagar Animal Rescue Centre
Jawahar Nagar
Srinagar
22 June 2016

Asha Khan
38 GK Marg
Srinagar

Dear Miss Khan,

Thank you for your letter of 6 June 2016 applying for a voluntary job at the Srinagar Animal Rescue Centre. A great deal of interest has already been shown in our request for volunteers, but we still have a few vacancies. We are looking for people who are enthusiastic about rehabilitating animals.

We would like to invite you to visit us on Friday 1 July at 10.30 a.m. to discuss the post and responsibilities. Please contact our veterinarian, Dr Sharma.

With best wishes,
Zubaida Singh
Srinagar Animal Rescue Centre

a. Where does Zubaida Singh work?

b. Why does Zubaida Singh invite Asha to visit the Srinagar Animal Rescue Centre?

c. What is the main purpose behind writing the letter?

d. Read each sentence. In the brackets, write **F** if it is a fact or **O** if it is an opinion.

   i. A great deal of interest has already been shown in our request for volunteers. [ ]

   ii. We still have a few vacancies. [ ]

e. What does **rehabilitating** mean? Tick the correct answer.

   i. bringing back to good health   ii. teaching good habits

f. Find and write down an adjective clause in the first paragraph of the letter.

 ISBN 978-93-5103-603-6

2. Read the story and answer the questions below in your notebook.

The Holiday Job

Suchi had a summer job at the museum. The work of helping the staff to reorganise the displays in the museum was very interesting. The display cases were emptied and their contents stored in locked cupboards. Then the cases were cleaned, dismantled and put together again in different shapes and positions. After that, the new displays were arranged inside them, and new labels printed and set beside the exhibits.

One day when Suchi was helping Dr Alva arrange a case of precious Japanese belt ornaments, something awful happened. Dr Alva had unlocked the cupboard and taken out six ornaments. As they were positioning the ornaments in the new display case, they found to their horror that there were only five. Suchi was afraid Dr Alva would suspect her of having taken the missing one.

However, he had no such suspicions. "Let's look carefully," he said. They returned to the store cupboard. Suchi bent down and looked under it. Thank goodness! There was the missing ornament. It had fallen and rolled underneath the cupboard. Dr Alva was happy, and Suchi was relieved that her chances of one day getting a proper job in the museum were not spoilt.

a. What do you think would have happened if the sixth ornament had not been found?
b. What is the main idea of the second paragraph?
c. What effect does the recovery of the missing ornament have on Suchi?
d. Write a summary of how Suchi and Dr Alva managed to find the missing ornament.
e. What does **dismantle** mean? Tick the correct answer.
   i. organise
   ii. take something to pieces

Spot the Error

f. There is a mistake in each sentence. Underline it and rewrite the sentence correctly.
   i. "Will I place these ornaments in the display case, Dr Alva?" asked Suchi.
   ii. As long as Suchi and Dr Alva discovered one ornament was missing, they began to look for it.
   iii. Suchi themselves found the missing ornament under the cupboard.
   iv. Suchi was too glad that the ornament was not lost.

 ISBN 978-93-5103-603-6

3. Use the outline below to write an e-mail to a friend.

greet your friend – thank them for their e-mail – invite them to join you on a trip to the seaside with your parents – say why you think it would be worth visiting the seaside – mention how excited you are and what preparations you are making – suggest a suitable date and place for meeting – add a good-bye note or greeting and sign off

 ISBN 978-93-5103-603-6

4. Use the outline below to write a story.

it is holiday time – Payal and her friend Khushi are playing on the beach – their parents have gone off for a stroll nearby – the lone lifeguard is busy talking on his mobile phone – the children build a sandcastle – they wade into the shallow water and climb on to some rocks nearby – they pretend they are shipwrecked sailors – suddenly they discover that the sea is too rough for them to swim back to the beach – they scream for help – the lifeguard throws them a couple of lifebuoys

  ISBN 978-93-5103-603-6

Word Power

Synonyms and antonyms

A synonym of any particular word is a word that means the same. For example, **merry** is a synonym of **cheerful**.

An antonym of any particular word is a word that means the opposite. For example, **bad** is the antonym of **good**.

1. Circle the word in the brackets that is a synonym of the underlined word.
   a. Mr Singh was a jolly fellow. (clever / cheerful)
   b. We have a lot of enthusiastic volunteers. (hard-working / keen)
   c. My uncle has always been considered a bit eccentric. (odd / stupid)
   d. It's always the crafty people that get their own way. (artistic / cunning)
   e. The film was most entertaining. (amusing / interesting)
   f. Meeta is cautious about spending money. (slow / careful)

2. Fill in the blank with a suitable antonym of the underlined word in each sentence.
   a. I'm not being funny. I'm being quite ___________.
   b. Here is a list of masculine nouns and here is a list of ___________ nouns.
   c. After last week's victory, the team are now facing ___________.
   d. The wide path they had been walking along entered a ___________ tunnel.
   e. The jury found him innocent, although he was really ___________.
   f. You are forbidden to use laptops in the exam, but you are ___________ calculators.

3. Look at each word pair. In the brackets, write **S** if they are synonyms or **A** if they are antonyms.
   a. strength – weakness [ ]
   b. ornament – decoration [ ]
   c. summit – base [ ]
   d. permission – consent [ ]

 ISBN 978-93-5103-603-6

Adjectives ending in -ous and -ious

Adjectives that end in **-ous** and **-ious** have a similar ending sound.

Adjectives ending in -ous		Adjectives ending in -ious	
adventurous	humorous	ambitious	precious
courageous	mischievous	glorious	religious
dangerous	monstrous	ingenious	serious
enormous	mountainous	luscious	studious
famous	vigorous	notorious	vicious

Fill in each blank with **-ous** or **-ious**.

a. You must take vigor________ exercise in order to keep fit.
b. The army won a glor________ victory.
c. On the table was a bowl of lusc________ -looking peaches.
d. Dr Crippen was a notor________ criminal.
e. We were confronted by a monstr________ creature.
f. Mrs Green had a class of rather mischiev________ children.
g. She was the victim of a vic________ attack.
h. Dilip was a quiet, stud________ boy.

The word pairs as...as, so...that, too...to

The word pair **as...as** is used for comparisons and similes. The word pair **so...that** is used for introducing a clause. The word pair **too...to** is used to say what prevents something from happening.

Fill in the blanks in each sentence with the correct word pair.

a. The moon is shining ________ bright ________ day!
b. Mr Mehta was ________ deaf ________ he didn't hear the fire alarm.
c. Sajid was ________ lazy ________ do his homework.
d. The pilot decided that it was ________ windy ________ take off safely.
e. My marks were ________ good ________ yours.
f. I was ________ nervous ________ I couldn't eat my breakfast.
g. Dipak has ________ good a chance ________ Hamid of getting into the team.
h. I've ________ many worries already ________ start worrying about grammar!

 ISBN 978-93-5103-603-6

Twin words

Certain pairs of words are always used in a fixed order. These words are called twin words.

1. Match the twin words with their meanings.

a. hale and hearty •	• i. spotlessly clean
b. pros and cons •	• ii. in good health
c. spick and span •	• iii. rules and customs
d. hustle and bustle •	• iv. occasionally
e. high and low •	• v. advantages and disadvantages
f. dos and don'ts •	• vi. everywhere
g. chalk and cheese •	• vii. noisy activity
h. now and then •	• viii. having many differences

2. Fill in the blanks with the correct twin words from the box below.

hale and hearty	now and then	high and low	dos and don'ts
spick and span	chalk and cheese	pros and cons	hustle and bustle

a. Mum looked ________________ for her glasses, but she couldn't find them.

b. Priya and Sri are the best of friends, even though they are as different as ________________.

c. The ________________ of the weekly market is colourful and fascinating.

d. Sandy has not been a professional swimmer for years but he still participates in local competitions ________________.

e. I hope you have looked at the ________________ before arriving at your decision?

f. Remember to read the ________________ before you visit a new country!

g. With three small children in the house, it is difficult to keep it ________________.

h. Although Grandfather is nearly a hundred, he's ________________.

 ISBN 978-93-5103-603-6

Idioms

Idioms are lively expressions that you use to make a strong point. They consist of images that communicate your meaning in an exaggerated way. For example, if you say, "It's no good **crying over spilt milk**", you mean it's no use getting upset about damage that has already been done and can't be undone. If you say that someone "**got his fingers burnt**", you mean that they took an unnecessary risk and suffered as a result.

1. Write in the blanks what you think is the meaning of the idioms underlined below.
   a. What's for dinner? I could eat a horse!

   ____

   b. The work won't take long. It'll be child's play!

   ____

   c. He told me out of the blue that he was getting married.

   ____

   d. We're wasting time chasing our own tails.

   ____

   e. Brinda always keeps a cool head in a crisis.

   ____

   f. Mukesh Sharma? That name rings a bell.

   ____

   g. The boss poured cold water on my idea.

   ____

2. Find an idiom in the box that matches the underlined words in each sentence. Put the idiom number in the brackets given.

1. call a spade a spade	2. couldn't keep a straight face
3. bending over backwards	4. not my cup of tea
5. on the dot	

Example He arrived punctually at 6.30 exactly. [5]

a. I'm a simple, straightforward person. I say frankly what I think. [ ]

b. Ballroom dancing is not something I enjoy. [ ]

c. They're trying very hard to help you. [ ]

d. It was very funny. I couldn't help laughing. [ ]

 ISBN 978-93-5103-603-6

Proverbs

A proverb is a wise saying that expresses a common fact or offers advice on how to live your life.

1. Match the proverbs with their meanings.

a. Every cloud has a silver lining.	• •	i. If you use your money and resources carefully, you won't be left in need.
b. Don't cross your bridges until you come to them.	• •	ii. If everybody helps, the job will be done quickly and easily.
c. Don't throw out the baby with the bathwater.	• •	iii. If you hurry a job, you'll make mistakes that slow you down.
d. Waste not, want not.	• •	iv. Make sure, in your enthusiasm for clearing stuff out, that you don't throw away the most important thing.
e. More haste, less speed.	• •	v. Don't worry about future decisions until you have to.
f. Many hands make light work.	• •	vi. You can always find something good about a bad situation.
g. Easier said than done.	• •	vii. It is difficult to stop performing familiar routines even when they are unnecessary.
h. A cat may look at a king.	• •	viii. People who appear quiet and dull may have hidden depths to their personalities.
i. The pen is mightier than the sword.	• •	ix. A course of action may be easy to talk about, but difficult to carry out.
j. Old habits die hard.	• •	x. The written word is more powerful than brute force.
k. Still waters run deep.	• •	xi. We are all equal – the humblest creatures need not feel awed by the most important.

 ISBN 978-93-5103-603-6

2. Read each story. Then write the proverb that it illustrates in the blank below.

a. Jay had applied for a job in a faraway part of the country. He was very upset when he didn't get it, and his brothers were sorry for him. At the same time they were delighted that he wouldn't be leaving them after all.

____

b. Kavita had a lot of homework to do, but wanted to go out and meet her friend Indu. So she did the work as quickly as she could. However, when she looked through it she found lots of mistakes and had to rewrite it. So she was too late and could not meet Indu.

____

c. There was so much to do for our housewarming party! Cooking, putting up the new curtains, vacuuming, getting fresh flowers for the vases. And then we had to make sure there were enough chairs for everybody to sit on! James, Brian and I pitched in to help Mum and Dad, and it was all done in no time!

____

d. I shouldn't have spent all my money shopping online! It's the end of the month now and I don't have enough left over to pay my medical bills.

____

e. Mira didn't do well in her exams and was sure she would fail. She decided she would give up studies altogether and look for a job instead. She told her family and friends about her decision. When the results were declared, she found she had passed after all! So she didn't need to look for a job.

____

f. Zubin used to be a quiet, studious boy at school. Nobody imagined he would grow up to be one of the most popular rock musicians in the country!

____

g. Sana thinks that she'll learn salsa and become a professional dancer in a few weeks. She has no idea how difficult the footwork is to learn.

____

 ISBN 978-93-5103-603-6